The Blizzard of '91

The BLIZZARD of '91

Clive Carter

DAVID & CHARLES
Newton Abbot

ISBN 0 7153 5137 0

COPYRIGHT NOTICE
© CLIVE CARTER 1971

Set in 11 on 12pt Janson
and printed in Great Britain
by Bristol Typesetting Company Limited
for David & Charles (Publishers) Limited
South Devon House   Newton Abbot   Devon

To my wife

Contents

List of Illustrations

CHARTS

1

In the path of the blizzard

> . . . *the wind was moaning sadly, and the sky as dark as a wood, and the straw in the yard swirling round and round, and the cows huddling into the great cowhouse, with their chins upon one another. But we, being blinder than they, I suppose, and not having had a great snow for years, made no preparation against the storm . . .*
>
> —R. D. Blackmore, *Lorna Doone*

It is Sunday evening, 8 March 1891. Country church bells are ringing above the north-east wind, carriages and traps pull up with clatter and creak, and pedestrians hurry between them, huddling into cloaks and shrugging collars around their ears because the weather has turned cold. The congregation's thoughts are not entirely with God. Tomorrow will be Monday again. Washday—the men will be away to work, and the worst of the winter's drying problem is over. For the lady in the family pew at the front, the problems are of a different kind—the servants take so much organising on a Monday. A farmer bows his head but at the back of his mind he worries; one of the horses is coughing and he had hoped to put the seed in Fiveacres tomorrow—lucky the season is so well advanced, most of the corn and potatoes already in before the weather turned so changeable. Behind him a middle-aged couple are thinking about their only son, at sea with his uncle, as they always do when the weather turns bad. But the wind will blow itself out tonight, the morning will be fine.

The morning was fine; but by evening the 'streets were deserted, all the traffic stopped; neither horse nor man could stand against the thick driving snow and the piercing wind.' The blizzard of '91 had come to an unsuspecting West Country.

Created by a freak weather condition which brought 20ft snowdrifts to the Devon lanes and froze sailors to death on the Cornish coast, the blizzard descended on a generation which, without aid of lorries, bulldozers, or helicopters, seemed ill-equipped to cope with sudden and widespread emergencies. But cope it did, for snow was just an extra trial and hazard of life in an age when the hardness of one's lot was tempered by an independence and self-sufficiency long since vanished. Farmers and cottagers relied little on towns; milk, butter, eggs, meat and greens came from their own acres, with only an occasional trip to stock up with groceries, oil, candles and sundries. If no coal was available, turf or furze could be burnt, and on the seacoast they and everybody else used driftwood. Even in towns all but the poorest housewife took pride in home preserves and a well-stocked larder.

One of the first effects of the blizzard was the total eclipse of traffic on the roads, though unlike the modern car, a horse had, and still has, the advantage that it can be unharnessed and led or ridden away from the blocked lanes and icy hills. Railways faced the ordeal of frozen points and signals and embedded trains during heavy snow, but they were kept running wherever possible by hard-working railwaymen. In 1891 there were only old-fashioned iron ram ploughs to cut through the drifts as the rotary plough was still in its infancy and the chief weapon in the winter arsenal of the Great Western and London & South Western railways was still the spade, wielded by the brawny arms of a ganger.

At sea, it was still the days when the safety of a ship, whether clipper or schooner, depended on the nose of her skipper for bad weather, the rise and fall of the glass, and the sharp eyes of her lookouts. There was no 'Now here is a gale warning...' from a friendly BBC, and a sudden storm often took a heavy toll of lives and ships.

One of the most terrifying aspects of the blizzard of 1891 was its devastating suddenness. A week of unsettled weather and a wet Sunday were followed by a fair Monday morning, when at an early hour, according to a contemporary report, 'the barometer had been rising slightly, and ... the day "promised to be fine" ... nothing was said about a great fall of snow, accompanied by a hurricane fierce enough to send it down in powder, without even allowing time for the formation of snowflakes'. Many farmers were caught with flocks and herds still up on the moors and high fields. They had perhaps four or five hours to round them up before nightfall, an impossible task for most of them despite heroic efforts of farmhands and shepherds. The result was a loss in Cornwall and Devon which must have totalled upwards of 6,000 sheep and lambs, a crippling blow to farmers who had also to make good losses of other animals, and damage wrought by the 90 mph gale to sheds, barns and orchards.

The blizzard claimed over 200 lives, the majority of which were lost at sea, where sixty-three known ships went down between the Goodwins and the Scilly Isles. On land, the destruction of trees was vast; over half a million, young and old, came down, and many forests and woodlands took generations to recover. Surprisingly, no one was killed by a falling tree, and the deaths on land were remarkably few considering the appalling conditions, the collapse of chimneys and roofs, and the many narrow escapes.

It was not the depth of snow in itself that was particularly dangerous, though it piled so high against houses that a common experience was that of a little girl and her brothers, living at Okehampton, who 'greatly enjoyed jumping out of the upstairs windows on to it', and there were rumours of cottages buried but for their chimneys. What made the blizzard a killer was the easterly hurricane, which rose at noon on the 9th and raged unabated until dusk on the 10th, making the snow fall

> ... in blinding sheets, not light flaky snow, such as poets like to sing about, but fine, powdery snow, that penetrated eyes and ears, made walking in the face of it next to an impossibility, and gradually piled up its tiny pellets into huge masses of a solid character many feet deep.[1]

It was the force of the wind that made cows turn round and walk tail first towards the home byre; sifted into every crack so that at one house at least it formed 'a thin, narrow column of snow *inside* the front door' from the floor to the keyhole where it had blown through; and, so the story went, bowled over two large men in a Plymouth street:

> Valiantly they strove to reach a friendly lamp-post, and to it they anchored themselves ... No sooner had the pair cast themselves adrift than the wind lifted them off their feet, and in an instant they lay sprawling in the snow. One of them stands six feet in his stockings, and is mighty of bulk; and the other is a good second to him. Yet the wind played with the prostrate giants, rolling them over and over, until they looked like a couple of enormous snowballs. Taking advantage of a brief lull, they rose, shook themselves out, and eventually reached a place of refuge in safety. Said No 2 to No 1: 'I didn't care much for the wind or the snow, but I was awfully

afraid of you, old boy; for if you had rolled over me you would have killed me!'[2]

But the more serious aspect of the gale was the bitter cold and violent disturbance it caused, almost the sole reasons for the deaths and the destruction. Without it

there would have been a great fall of snow . . . but it would have been a snowstorm and not a blizzard, and many of the phenomenal aspects of the visitation under notice would have been absent.[3]

Although there were some fanciful theories put forward as to the cause of the 'visitation', this distinction between a snowstorm and a blizzard is still the same. In a blizzard the snow, which need not be very heavy, though it often is especially in severe conditions, is accompanied by strong winds leading to drifting. A depression is caused by warm, moist air rising; the greater the rate of ascent of air, the deeper the depression, and the stronger the winds around it and the moister the air, the heavier the fall of rain or snow. Snow itself is formed in the same way as most of the rain in this country, initially at great height in the atmosphere where temperatures are such that water is normally in the frozen state. Whether, when the frozen particles fall, they reach the ground as snow or rain depends simply on the temperature in the lowest layers of the atmosphere determining whether melting can take place. If the low-level winds are such that the air is below freezing point, snow results, and the more these factors are exaggerated, the more severe are the blizzard conditions.

In the south-west of England a typical blizzard weather system is a depression approaching from the direction of the Azores, passing over warm seas and arriving off the coast as a warm, very moist mass of air. If the depression moves up the English Channel and is sufficiently deep, strong winds can result which may well be from an easterly direction, feeding cold low-level air from the

Continent into the low-pressure area. Thus there are strong low-level winds, cold low-level air, and relatively very warm moist air aloft at the levels where precipitation takes place, and the most likely cause of heavy snow and drifting in the south-west.

In 1891 'blizzard' itself was a new term, an Americanism which came into sudden and popular usage that week, having first arrived in England only a month before when a severe snowstorm was reported in Nebraska. The Union Pacific Railroad between Cheyenne and Sydney was blocked, and six mail or express trains with upwards of 500 passengers were snowed up for two days. Little was it thought that the GWR and LSWR in Britain were soon to face similar conditions as the Union Pacific, and on the same date as a further blizzard was to sweep the states of Iowa, Illinois, Ohio and Minnesota.

Unexpected as the West Country blizzard was, it had been preceded by the greatest frost since 1740, when

all the lakes in England froze; and a whole ox was roasted on the Thames. Many trees were killed by the frost; and postilions were benumbed on their saddles... the General Assembly of the Church of Scotland ordained a national fast to be held on account of the dearth which then prevailed.[4]

In 1716 fairs were held on the frozen Thames, and 'printers and booksellers pursued their professions on its surface', and in the great winter of 1684, immortalised by Blackmore in *Lorna Doone*, coaches drove along the Thames, where the ice was a foot thick, most of the hollies were killed and even the oaks split by the frost, and very few birds survived. That the Thames did not freeze like this in 1891 was not due to less severe weather, so much as to the fact that its freezing was caused by the narrow arches of Old London Bridge slowing the current before its demolition in 1832.

Scotland suffered such great winters more frequently,

though there is an eighteenth-century record of a woman buried in a snowdrift near Yeovil, in Somerset, for seven days, before she was dug out alive. In 1620 the 'thirteen drifty days' passed into Scottish legend, when it snowed for thirteen days and nights, with an almost total loss of sheep, and in 1795 whole flocks were buried in a few hours by drifting snow, and seventeen shepherds died. After the thaw, and the subsidence of the resultant floods, there were found

> where the tide of the Solway throws up what has been brought into it by the rivers, the carcasses of 1,840 sheep, nine black cattle, three horses, two men, one woman, forty-five dogs, and a hundred and eighty hares, besides a number of smaller animals.[5]

Here is mentioned something that seems to have been entirely overlooked in the 1891 records, the effect of the blizzard on wild life. In those days there was no enthusiastic counting or ringing of wild animals and birds, and few people cared whether they existed at all, except perhaps to hunt them. Most species were far more plentiful then than now, and if any emotion were felt at a massacre it was likely to be delight at being rid of a great number of 'pests'; in those days of the gin trap only the eccentric or the misguided cared about the welfare of wild creatures.

Only word-of-mouth records have come to light, to the effect that nearly all the rabbits and birds died, and that the birds could be seen hanging, frozen, in the branches of the trees. If other hard winters are any guide, the mortality among birds must have been great; even in an ordinarily severe frost many of the smaller species die. As far back as AD 545 the birds allowed themselves to be caught by the hand, and as recently as 1962, when the author was working in the royal dockyard, Devonport, a seagull was so frozen and weak with starvation that it fell dead from the sky on to the deck of HMS *Plymouth*.

The blizzard of 1891 must also have killed vast numbers of the smaller animals, particularly those which live on the ground, such as hares. Badgers and other hibernating species may have been brought out by the fine February weather, but in all probability just went back to sleep for a while. Perhaps the hardest hit in comparison with their numbers must have been the red deer on Exmoor, which would have suffered the same fate and the same casualties as the sheep, cattle and ponies on the moor.

The Continent has always been more prone to spectacular winters than the British Isles. In AD 462, Theodomer marched over the frozen Danube to avenge his brother's death in Swabia; in 763 not only the Black Sea but the Strait of Dardanelles was frozen over, the snow was fifty feet deep in places, and the heaps of ice in the cities pushed down the walls, and in 860 the Adriatic was frozen. In 1133 the Po was frozen from Cremona to the sea and it is recorded that 'the wine casks were burst, and even the trees split by the action of the frost, with immense noise.' In 1236 the Danube was frozen to the bottom, and in 1292 the Rhine bore loaded waggons. 'One sheet of ice extended between Norway and Jutland, so that travellers passed with ease; and in Germany 600 peasants were employed to clear away the snow for the advance of the Austrian army.'[6]

Campaigning was evidently hard in those days; in 1468, it is said, 'the winter was so severe in Flanders that the wine distributed to the soldiers was cut in pieces with hatchets'. In 1658 Charles X of Sweden crossed the Little Belt over the ice from Holstein to Denmark, with his whole army, foot and horse, followed by the train of baggage and artillery, and in 1792 French Republican dragoons galloped across the frozen Texel to seize the Dutch fleet.

The year of 1891 was the 900th anniversary of another severe winter, when 'famine and pestilence closed the year', and exactly 200 years since, in 1691, the cold in Vienna had been so intense that famished wolves had entered the city and attacked cattle, and even men. In 1891 not wolves but jackals were driven down to ravage flocks in the villages around Malaga. The Tagus was frozen up to Toledo, and at Saragossa the Ebro was covered with fifteen inches of ice. Europe was frozen from the Baltic to the Adriatic; the river Soan iced over at Lyons and the Rhône as far up as Arles. Every major river of the Continent was blocked, and the port of Antwerp was closed by ice. Marseilles docks were frozen over, Cannes was snowbound, and the fountains of Nice were glittering tiers of ice. The lakes of Constance, Morat and Zurich were solid, and five inches of snow lay in the streets of Naples. On 20 January a sudden thaw set in, the east wind backed westerly and the temperature went up to 40 degrees Fahrenheit. Serious flooding resulted, particularly in the estuaries of the Somme and the Rhine, where sappers had to dynamite massive jams of ice to allow the rivers to flow.

The great frost in England set in towards the end of November 1890, and by Christmas the Serpentine in London's Hyde Park, the Welsh Harp at Hendon and the ponds around Hampstead and Highgate were covered by six inches of ice. The fen country in eastern England was frozen over, and the Lincolnshire Skating Association organised a long-distance race on the river Welland; the new sport of tobogganing was much in vogue on the Surrey downs, but in the London slums the bitter weather brought severe distress to the poor and unemployed. In Hertfordshire a christening party, complete with god-parents, made its way along the ice of the then Grand Junction Canal to Apsley, on 18 January 1891.

In Devon, a small girl on a visit to Chagford was invited to join a small party of relatives to see the skating which was daily taking place at Cranmere Pool.

When we reached the spot there indeed were the skaters enjoying themselves. Also on the thick ice cups of hot tea were being prepared for any and everybody to consume ... the lady in charge of this tea-making invited our driver to lead on the pony and trap which brought us. This he did, to everybody's delight, for, she said, 'Such an experience may never happen again'.[7]

The cold, crisp days of January were succeeded by a February of 'fine, genial, spring-like weather', so dry and warm that it caused a state of drought in parts of Cornwall and Devon, and remained as long in the memory as the blizzard itself. Bright new butterflies fluttered about and spring flowers bloomed, though in this strange season the New Year had already seen primroses at Fowey and daisies at Trevone, in spite of the cold, and roses had been gathered at Christmas.

By the end of the month the *Royal Cornwall Gazette* reported that 'agriculturalists have seldom had a finer February for spring sowings and seldom have they got so much grain into the ground by March 2nd, as they have this year.' In the gardening column, the same issue remarked 'the continual fine and dry weather enables us to proceed with out-door work of all descriptions.' People in their nineties could not recall such a beautiful February, and there were hopes of an early and abundant harvest.

With the opening of March the weather became unsettled, but still remained dry. Friday 6 March dawned fair, but the barometer was falling and the day grew overcast, and though there were still occasional periods of sunshine it was getting colder. On the Saturday it was very overcast and much-needed rain fell fairly steadily until the evening, as the cold front advancing southwards across the British Isles began to show signs of waving. By Sunday the front had moved south, but a small depression was passing across the western counties and causing frequent rain. During the night the wind had backed from west to east, and throughout the day it freshened strongly and steadied at north-east. It had become very cold as air reached Cornwall from the far north, but still there was no anticipation of the unprecedented blizzard that was to come. (See Appendix 1, Weather Charts).

So it has been with every severe winter, and so it will perhaps always be, though with our modern weather reporting we should be better prepared than those who read *The Times* forecast for the south-west on Monday 9 March 1891; 'North-easterly winds, moderate; fair generally.'

2

Monday: dawn to dusk

*The storm had come in good earnest, and promised to
be no trifling one.*
> —E. Wetherell, *The Wide Wide World*

Monday 9 March 1891 dawned as many another cold
winter's day, unusual only in that, at that date in the West
Country, it should have been spring. There was no indication of the coming storm, especially as around 8 am the
barometer had risen slightly and the strong easterly wind
had moderated, but as the morning progressed people all
over Devon and Cornwall began to feel that a 'fall of something' was imminent. Some knowingly reached for their
copy of *Old Moore's Almanack* with its prediction of
heavy snow for March, and the real pessimists mulled over
newspaper reports of the havoc brought by the recent
Nebraskan blizzard.

Most people, however, went about their business, sheltering from the sharp rain and sleet squalls, and not until 11
am did they notice that the wind was rising again. By
noon it was 'blowing lustily from the NE and heavy clouds
lined the eastern sky' above Dartmoor. An hour later the
vanguard of the blizzard swept up the Channel.

Out to sea captains who had been encouraged by the lull at daylight to resume their voyages were soon tossing in rough seas. One large fleet of sail which had spent the night behind Plymouth breakwater dispersed as vessel after vessel ran for shelter. Padstow ketches, Fowey schooners and French *chassemarées* stormed into Fowey, Charlestown and Mevagissey; in their wake sailed luggers, drivers and pilot gigs, all flying before what was now expected to be a very bad blow from the east. Some coasters, too far out to make the land, held to their courses, among them the tiny wooden smack *Dove* of Topsham, owned by George Hurdle, coal and manure merchant, which had left Exmouth Bight on Sunday evening, in ballast for Gweek on the Helford river. Though stoutly built, the *Dove* sprang a serious leak, and in the freshening gale off Dodman Capt Edward Trout, standing to the wheel with mate Frederick Rowe, was flung overboard. He seized a trailing rope and hauled himself back on board, numb and shivering. Both men resumed the struggle to keep the crippled smack before the gale, and as heavy seas continually swept her, the mate's thirteen-year-old son was battened down in the

'Vessel after vessel ran for shelter'

cabin. Around 1 pm it began to snow, thin powdery stuff which whirled lightly in the gusts, the first fall of the great blizzard.

During a lull the two men recognised the jagged cliffs flanking the Manacles, off the western tip of Falmouth Bay, but the *Dove* was already far enough to leeward to clear the reef, and had a chance of reaching Helford estuary, only three miles distant. Anxiously watching her from the fishing village of Porthoustock was James Henry Treloar Cliff, second coxswain of the lifeboat. At thirty-three he was already a veteran seaman who had started his career in local pilchard boats and then graduated to the old wooden-walled naval training ship *Ganges* at Falmouth. Invalided out of the Royal Navy at Devonport, he had gone back to the fisherman's trade, though sailing deep water and coastal if the season was bad. On this particular Monday morning Cliff had been in his cottage making a mat before going up to do some gardening at St Keverne vicarage, when his mother ran in with news that a storm was brewing. He joined other fishermen on Porthoustock beach, and they were alarmed to see the little *Dove* come thrashing towards the land. Capt Trout hauled to windward on the port tack, but the jib halliards parted and Cliff knew the smack would not clear the Levellers reef. Off came the fishermen's caps, and in obedience to their frantic waving Trout put his helm up and headed for the beach. For several long minutes the *Dove* lay poised below the cliffs, then struck bows-on.

Porthoustock had its own lifeboat, the eight-oared self-righting *Charlotte*, but Cliff made for the coil of rope and lifebuoy kept in a small shed under the capstan house. Discarding the cumbersome belt, he slipped the rope about his waist, handed the end to his friends and plunged into the waves. As he got under the smack's bows the boy was thrown down to him, and the men ashore hauled away with a will, dragging both underwater but landing them safely.

Cliff paused for breath, then went out for the mate, and again rescuer and rescued were hauled off their feet through the waves. After a third foray had brought Capt Trout spluttering to the shingle, he and the mate were shepherded up to Cliff's cottage by his mother, while the boy was taken care of by a neighbour.

Hardly had this excitement died down than, at 2 pm, some men from Rosenithon, a hamlet overlooking the Manacles, ran down the hill to Porthoustock with news that a pair of ketches were jammed on the lee shore just northward of Godrevy Cove. Their plight, which had been hidden from the covers by the high land of Manacle Point, was grave, as the tide, driven by the gale, was already fast flooding. James Hill, coxswain of the *Charlotte*, fired maroons for his crew, but some of the regulars did not arrive and others were understandably reluctant to make what was rapidly becoming a suicidal attempt to launch her. A score of fishermen, the indomitable Cliff among them, seized ropes and ran out to the headland above Godrevy Cove, only to see one of the ketches part her cable and be driven ashore. Her crew swam desperately but only one man crawled on to a flat rock, and he was swept away even as Cliff scrambled down towards him. The other ketch broke loose soon afterwards, and though the fishermen waved her towards Porthkerris Cove, she struck and foundered without a single survivor.

Though Cliff and his fellows did not know it, they had just witnessed the end of the 54-ton dandy ketch *Aquilon* of Jersey, John Foster master, wheat-laden from Plymouth to Bristol, and the Portsmouth ketch *Catherine*, manned by Capt George Bowden and his youngest son Harry, bound for Truro with nitrate of soda, both vessels having sailed with the coaster fleet from Plymouth that morning. Capt Bowden's eldest son, master of the ketch *Friendship*, entered Falmouth from Par only two hours after the tragedy and, anxious about his father and brother, had wired back to Plymouth for news of them. There was none, and word of the Manacle wrecks was not to reach Falmouth for another two days; even then the *Catherine* was at first wrongly identified as the *Edwin*, until this ketch, whose skipper had put back off Rame Head, was discovered moored snugly in Millbay Docks.

The easterly gale was also howling out beyond Land's End, and already at noon the Scilly packet *Lyonesse*, outward bound from Penzance, had encountered off Wolf Rock the 98-ton Cardigan schooner *Martha*, three days out from Caernarvon to London with slates. Dismasted, and with water over the cabin floor, she was settling fast, but Capt Hooper dared not launch a boat and the schooner's own had been swept away. Eventually, after much careful manoeuvring, he backed the *Lyonesse* under the *Martha's* counter, and repeated this hazardous performance four times as, one after the other, the four life-jacketed Welshmen leaped to safety. They were landed at St Mary's at 4 pm, leaving the doomed schooner to disappear into the thickening curtain of snow.

A dozen miles away the 140-ton iron steamer *Stannington* of Southampton, bound from Ardglass to Exeter with potatoes, snapped her tail-shaft while steaming into the rough seas. Auxiliary sail was hoisted and blown away, but she was in no immediate danger unless swept among the Scilly rocks, and after hoisting distress flags her crew settled down to await a tug or help from a passing steamer.

By 3 pm the snow was bad enough to drive the broccoli-cutters and potato-planters from the fields above Gulval and Marazion, while across Mount's Bay ship after ship was rounding up into the shelter of Penzance pier. The *Old Hound*, the *Desdemona*, the *John and Robert*, and the *Mary Elizabeth*, took the harbour sands; behind them came the local steamer *Gervase*, which had battled around Land's End with a general cargo from Bristol. There had already been one moment of excitement when the crew of the

Brixham trawling sloop *Courage*, who had landed their catch by punt, nearly capsized while trying to return aboard. The coastguards were called out, but the fishermen were saved by a pilot gig.

Yet another battered schooner arrived on the flood tide, the *Gorey Lass* of Jersey, coal-laden from Cardiff to Roscoff, and early in the evening the Bude ketch *Purveyor* came in, bringing dire news. At noon, off Longships, she had met another Bude coaster, the 59-ton *Agnes*, Samuel Rowlands master, a day out from Britonferry to Devoran with culm. The *Purveyor* was in no position to help, and the *Agnes* had fallen away to leeward.

This report increased fears for the 105-ton Penzance schooner *Prima Donna*, which had left Porthcawl for home with coal on Sunday morning. Although she was quite old, having been launched at Llanelly in 1851, Capt Smith was an experienced seaman, and his crew comprised mate Crocker and able seamen Bluett, Bickford and Cronin, all well-known and competent local sailors. Another Cornish schooner, the *Rose* of Gerrans, two days out from Lydney to St Mawes with coal, had been glimpsed tacking through the snow off the Longships. On board were her genial and much-respected master, Thomas Peters, his son, and two sailors, Pascoe and Lampshire, all of whom had families awaiting their safe return to Gerrans.

But it was not only small sailing ships that had been caught by the blizzard; off the Welsh coast HMS *Neptune*, the Holyhead guardship, bound for Portsmouth for the prize firing, had been forced to heave-to by very heavy seas. The 3,000-ton Hamburg-Amerika liner *Seuvia* was also in trouble off the coast of South Devon. She had left New York on 26 February, with eleven cabin and fifty steerage passengers, mostly Hungarians, Russians and Bohemians returning home from the American mines. Fine weather and a fresh southerly breeze had graced the voyage until two o'clock that morning, when she passed the Lizard in rough hazy weather. It worsened, and at 3 pm off Prawle Point the passengers were alarmed by a 'great crash above the roar of the wind.' The piston of the *Seuvia's* LP cylinder had broken, and she was left helpless. Capt Ludwig soon calmed his excited passengers and ordered a lower topsail and staysail set to take the liner off the land, though as a precaution he had the boats swung out.

The *Seuvia* drifted back down Channel, her decks battered by hailstones, and towards 6 pm St Elmo's Fire lit up the masts with a brilliance that Capt Ludwig, who had seen the phenomenon several times, had never previously witnessed. At 8 pm the leadsman sounded ten fathoms, and though the captain knew they were close to land again there was nothing he could do except run before the gale and keep his navigation lights burning brightly to reduce the serious danger of collision.

A hundred miles up the English Channel, the gale was playing havoc among the shipping moored inside the threequarter-mile curve of the Admiralty pier at Dover. Mountainous seas laden with shingle and boulders had been sweeping over the quays all afternoon, washing away baggage trollies, luggage and boat davits, as well as flooding offices and the railway lines which ran out to the packet berths. Two Rye smacks were driven hard against the sea wall, and another was carried from the centre of the harbour into the jetty, but harbourmaster Durden and two dockers secured her and rescued the cabin boy, who was the only person on board. Nearby, the London & Chatham Railway Company's paddler *Wave* broke loose and rolled so far over that her bilge keel was visible. During one violent yaw she splintered her starboard paddlebox, and an hour elapsed before a tug fetched her back to the inner quay.

Into this chaos, at 5 pm, steamed the Paris Club Train on her regular and luxurious run from Charing Cross.

Hauled by a handsome express engine, she rumbled on to the Admiralty pier, the spray dashing over the olive green coachwork and the brightly polished fittings. Among the passengers who alighted on to the wet, seaweed-strewn platform were the Duchess of Edinburgh and Lady Rothschild, who hurried on board the South Eastern Company's mail packet *Petrel*. They soon regretted their decision, and asked to be put ashore again. This took over an hour to accomplish, and though the *Petrel* was then replaced by the company's large packet *Victoria*, the duchess abandoned all idea of crossing to Calais that day, and with Lady Rothschild and thirty other passengers retired to the nearby Lord Warden Hotel. They still could not altogether escape the effect of the storm, however, as already large blocks of granite and York stone were being washed away from the hotel's windward side.

The storm was also making conditions inland very difficult, and those who could stayed indoors—so many, in fact, that a young medical student named Shepherd, walking down London's Regent Street at three o'clock in the afternoon, met not another soul in its entire length, and even Piccadilly Circus was deserted. At about the same time, over two hundred miles away in the West Country, schoolchildren released early because of the blizzard were having a hard struggle to reach home. One eleven-year-old pupil at Sparkwell school found the snow was about a foot deep by the time he reached home, and a Totnes Grammar School boy, in walking over the river bridge, had difficulty in fighting his way across against the wind and snow was frozen on his face by the time he reached his home in Bridgetown. In West Cornwall the elderly master of the church school at the village of Crowan dismissed his pupils around 3 pm, and even as early as that one nine-year-old only managed to reach his home because the last stretch lay under a leeward hedge.

The sudden descent of the blizzard also caught a great

many tradesmen and carters on the road, among them a young man who worked at a corn mill at Crickapit Farm in the parish of Bradoc.

The miller said 'Weather looks bad, Tommy—you'd better take the flour to the outlying farms in case a storm hinders you for a day or two.' By the time (he) had delivered his last bag and started back for home the snow was falling heavily. It became so bad he could hardly keep his eyes open but trusted to his horses to find the way home and just kept his hand on the shaft of the miller's cart. It was dark by the time he reached the mill, and the miller and his wife had been very worried and were greatly relieved to see him.[1]

Even in the sheltered suburbs of Plymouth the storm brought distress to travellers on foot. One wine merchant, J. R. Wilson of the Octagon,

was in the habit of hiring a horse-drawn victoria to come for a late lunch to his home, Thorn Park House at Mannamead . . . he had to travel uphill most of the way. If indeed he did get a victoria for the beginning of the journey, he was lucky, for most carts and carriages were off the streets, owing to the snow already fallen by 3 pm, and more especially to the freezing winds. (He) was 41 years, always a portly man, and simply had to make the best of a difficult journey home, and was so fatigued and out of breath that he crawled on his hands and knees the last half mile from Mutley Plain up over Townsend Hill to his home. When he got there his beard and moustache tinkled with the icicles hanging from them. How glad the family must have been to see him, for the screaming of the blizzard could be heard indoors.[2]

By 4 pm the gale which had already brought havoc to Dover and wrecks to the Manacles was gusting at over 50 mph; in Plymouth Sound a party of boys from HMS

Foudroyant were driven ashore in their longboat on Cawsand beach. Further up the coast at Start Point, the tip of the great wedge of South Devon jutting out into the Channel, coastguards were keeping vigilant watch as vessel after vessel dodged in and out of the bay under close-reefed sails. A lone brig, two schooners, and a large full-rigger behind a tug were sighted, then a tiny fishing hooker dashing for home. These were clear of the coast between the Dart estuary and Berry Head, but at 4.30 pm a large, single-stack steamer appeared in a more dangerous position off the Skerries, a long shoal running north-east of Start Point. She edged clear, though coastguards at the fishing village of Hallsands thought that her steering gear might be giving trouble, as she wallowed close to the land several times before steaming out of sight.

At 5.30 Mary Jane Briggs, wife of the second keeper of the Start light, saw the same steamer only a few hundred yards off the point. She ran to an upper window as the vessel struck full on the Blackstone reef and fell broadside to the waves. At once the hull parted abaft the bridge, the funnel and masts fell, the stern capsized into deep water, and the bows sank in a swirl of foam.

3

Monday night on the railways

. . . a very eventful episode in one's life, never to be forgotten, and, I may hope, never to be repeated.
—Frederick Townshend, quoted in *Doidge's Annual*

By early Monday evening snow blowing off the high moors of Devon and Cornwall had blocked railway cuttings and tunnel mouths, choked points, and was soon smothering any engine, broad or narrow gauge, which tried to push through the deepening drifts. This was especially so in Devon, where both the main GWR and LSWR lines traversed the bleak foothills of Dartmoor, one of the storm centres of the blizzard that night. Hardly a train had arrived at Plymouth North Road station, or Millbay, the ocean terminal, or the LSWR's Devonport Junction, since mid-afternoon, and as the evening drew on neither the crack GWR 'Zulu' express, nor any of the up Cornish mails appeared. Only an hour behind the 'Zulu' was another down express, the 'Flying Dutchman'; among her 200 passengers was the tall, bearded figure of the Duke of Edinburgh, bound for Devonport, whose wife had already been held up by the blizzard at Dover. Fears for the Paddington trains increased when rumours flew that the GWR

The Great Western Railway's 'Zulu' express snowed up alongside the down platform at Brent

Page 34

An unusually artistic photo-graph for its day shows a snowbound Penzance during the lull in the blizzard on the morning of Wednesday, 11 March 1891

line at Dawlish, where it skirts the shore of Torbay, had been demolished by huge seas.

Already at 4 pm the telegraph between Plymouth and Tavistock had been cut by falling trees, and by 7 pm communications with all stations to London had failed. An hour later the Cornish wires went dead, and the GWR divisional superintendent, C. C. Compton, with other officials, set off in a pilot engine through Plymouth's western suburbs towards Saltash, to discover how serious was the disruption of the telegraph service. At 9 pm they returned tender-first, defeated by a massive tangle of poles, wires and fir trees which the gale had strewn across the approaches to the Weston Mills trestle viaduct. Soon after this incident came news of the fast deteriorating conditions on Dartmoor. The LSWR 'Jubilee' express arrived several hours late from Waterloo, and her driver reported that near the moorland town of Okehampton he had forged through cuttings where the snow was half way up the driving wheels.

This boded ill for working the main LSWR line to Exeter and the GWR branch to Launceston. They left Plymouth separately but both tracks twisted through the steep river valleys of the Tamar and the Tavy to converge on Tavistock, and then side by side climbed the windswept western flank of Dartmoor to Lydford Junction, where the GWR turned away into the north Cornish moors, and the LSWR curved eastwards towards Okehampton.

It was from the Launceston branch that the first call for help came, when a light engine ran into Millbay with the news that the evening train was embedded in a great drift somewhere between Tavistock and the village of Horrabridge. One of her unlucky passengers was Mr Frederick Weekes, ARAM, a professor of music from Plymouth, who had left Mutley station by the early morning train to visit his pupils at Tavistock. Not liking the look of the weather, he had worn his thick overcoat and boots, and left his violin at home. By the time he reached his destination it was snowing hard, and by early evening the weather was very bad indeed.

At about 6.30 pm Mr Weekes left the home of Miss Fanny Cox, one of his pupils, though her mother pleaded with him to stay the night because of the blizzard, 'but fearing Lizzie would be anxious I determined to push on, saying "If the train goes I go".' As he ran down the hill, he was alarmed by a tremendous roaring noise which he took to be the river Tavy in flood and feared that the bridge might be down. When at last he reached it, he found he 'could not see any river in the blinding snow', and that the noise was the hurricane tearing through trees beside the bridge. Pressing on to the GWR station above the town, he stood in front of a blazing fire in the waiting-room to thaw himself out and by the time he had steamed dry the 6.10 pm branch train from Launceston had arrived. The rest of that evening's ordeal is best told in Mr Weekes's own words.

Off started the train going slowly. I was just comfort-ably settling myself in a corner with my back to the engine when crash came something against the window which made me jump back. There were two men in the same compartment and whilst each suggested what it was that struck the carriage window there came another and more determined crash sweeping the window and clearing the snow that had gathered on the pane. [These were trees falling around the train.] It was so dark that all we saw was something white which we supposed was the bank. Soon after getting on the viaduct we stopped, we heard afterwards that the driver had to get off the engine and saw away a fir tree that had fallen in front of the engine. No joke to get down from the engine in such a terrific storm, the very train trembled. [This tree fell on the southern end of the Magpie viaduct, so the train halted while the coaches were still on the middle.]

On we went again across the shaky viaduct as fast as we could, and then pulling up went at walking pace when down came another tree falling between engine and the carriage. We rose up as if about to leap a five-barred gate, in an instant the powerful brakes were put on and we came to a standstill. One of my companions rushed to the door and away flew his hat and he jumped out and came back with it. The driver got off his engine, lamp in hand. 'You're here for the night,' he cried. He went back to consult with the guard of the train and took ten minutes to reach the engine again. He had to try twenty times at least, before he could stand against the wind and the fine drifting snow. He unhooked the engine, telling us he must drive to Horrabridge. In about threequarters of an hour he returned, having had to get off his engine and remove trees about six times. He told us to get out and he would take us to Horrabridge on the engine. I was one of the first to jump out and was immediately up to my waist in snow which I ploughed through and working against wind and blinding snow I reached the engine. Fourteen of us were wedged up on the engine.

Crossing the long viaduct [Walkham, 130ft above the river] was awful. It really seemed as if we should be lifted up bodily and thrown over and then when we came to a deep cutting the snow rushed up as through a funnel. The fine snow coming up from beneath, the steam coming down on us from above, the howling wind and noise of the engine—we held our breath and wondered what would come next.

At last we reached the Horrabridge station. The snow had gathered so thickly on my spectacles that I was practically blind, and was about to step down between the engine and the platform, when someone cried out

'Not there—step right on to the platform.' I shouted 'I cannot see where the platform is—help me!' Immediately strong arms laid hold of me each side and voices cried 'Jump!' so I jumped blindly and landed in snow and was led into the waiting-room.

There was a roaring fire. I first wiped my spectacles and found my overcoat all frozen stiff. I took it off and dried it, in fact dried myself all over. In about two hours a second lot of passengers arrived, making about eighteen or twenty of us. It soon became apparent that we were there for the night, and we made the best of it. The porter said it was impossible for us to get down into the village for food or lodgings, there being drifts 14ft deep. He struggled down to his cottage about 100 yards off, getting once up to the neck in snow. He brought us back ¾lb of tea and a loaf of bread. We made tea in a dirty little teapot and drank milkless and sugarless tea out of a still dirtier mug, one mug serving for all. Later on the stationmaster and another official started for their cottages and three or four gentlemen of our party ventured to fight their way down to the hotel but could only get one small bed. We remained all night in the waiting-room, walking up and down, going sometimes into the next room, the ticket-office, for a change. It was a change for the worse, the floor being covered with pools of water from the drifting snow. Sleep seemed out of the question. Much of the night was spent in argument. The driver seemed a most intelligent man and so was the porter, only rather pigheaded. These two argued away for hours much to our amusement. On the walls were some striking texts 'A man shall be a hiding place from the wind' and others on the second coming of Our Lord.

Here we leave the passengers of the 6.10 train to their uncomfortable night at Horrabridge station, and return to

Stranded trains in Devon during the blizzard week

Tavistock, where the fight was continuing to keep points and signals free from snow and ice. Once porters and gangers ran for cover as a tall elm came crashing down into the yard, landing where only minutes before a horse and cart had stood. The last Launceston branch train arrived at 9.30 pm and was held, though steam was kept up. Her three passengers were accommodated at the nearby Railway Hotel.

On the lines above Tavistock the situation was worsening hourly; six miles away, near Lydford Junction, which, at nearly 1,000ft above sea level, was the highest and bleakest station on Dartmoor, lay the remnants of a goods train. Even before she reached Tavistock a heavy gust had stove in the doors of a fish van and torn off the sides and roof, scattering the big crates far and wide. Only the bare wheelbase was left when she ran into the station, but her crew, typical of every railwayman that night, resolutely carried on. They lost half the train in a cutting, before plunging into a massive block with only three wagons left, below the village of Bridestowe.

Two miles beyond the abandoned goods was the 6.38 pm slow train from Exeter (Queen Street). She had cleared Okehampton at eight o'clock, crossed the spidery 100ft lattices of the Meldon viaduct, and run safely through the junction. Speed fell off as she climbed Sourton bank, and ten minutes later, still steaming hard, she ran into a heavy drift in Youlditch cutting. Guard Moore, driver Bennetts and fireman Oats tried to dig her out, but failed. The guard struggled back to Meldon Junction and telegraphed to Exeter for help, but the two relief engines got no farther than a mile from the embedded train before they too became stuck. Meanwhile Moore and the engine crew had shut two women and their children in a warm first-class compartment, and they and seven men retired to the bitterly cold confines of the brake van.

High up on Dartmoor another engine crew were wielding shovels as, buffeted and almost blinded by the blizzard, they tried to free the evening branch train from Princetown village. The eight passengers had been told before the train left for Yelverton Junction that their through tickets to Plymouth were no guarantee of arrival, and they were soon regretting their rashness. Snow beat in around the closed windows and ventilators of the single composite coach even after they had been stuffed with scarves and handkerchiefs. Several times the engine pushed through deep drifts, but after covering only two miles she went into a huge block in Eggworthy cutting on bleak Walkhampton Common.

No amount of digging could clear the little tank's wheels, and the guard set off for Dousland village, three miles away. It might as well have been three hundred. An hour later, frozen and exhausted, he staggered back, so helplessly lost that he found the train by sheer chance. Nothing remained but to await the dawn, and engine crew and passengers huddled into a single compartment, wet, hungry, and numb with the cold. At 7 am the oil lamp went out, leaving them in total darkness; an hour later the guard, reinforced by the fireman, again waded off through the drifts towards Dousland. Soon after they left, the driver, though suffering from exposure, set off in their footsteps, limping with an injury received while trying to free the engine. The hapless passengers remained packed together, hoping for rescue, and not knowing their ordeal was to last for another sixteen hours.

If the telegraph lines eastward of Plymouth had not been broken in half a dozen places, the GWR officials would have learned the same dismal story of stranded trains, though they did have an early warning of the terrible conditions along the southern edge of Dartmoor. Mr Compton, after his return from Camel's Head, had taken another pilot engine out beyond Plympton, but could get no further against the blizzard. Not long afterwards, at 1.30

am, the evening up London mail rumbled back into Millbay station. Barely making headway against the hurricane, she had climbed the steep two miles of Hemerdon bank, to be confronted by a cutting almost blocked by a drift. The engine crew demurred at trying to pound their way through, shunted around to the rear, and with considerable clashing of buffers extricated the train and set off tender-first back to Plymouth. As the passengers crowded into the waiting rooms or crossed the road to the Duke of Cornwall Hotel, they little realised how lucky they were compared with those on board another up London mail which had preceded their train out of Millbay at 6.30 pm. She went up Hemerdon bank and then waited threequarters of an hour for a down express to pass, and had cleared Cornwood when passengers heard the rasp of fallen telegraph wires on the carriage roofs. Seconds later a violent jerk flung them into disarray. The engine was derailed and they were marooned in Langham cutting.

A small party of engineers and gangers arrived but only four passengers chose to go with them to nearby Ivybridge. The remaining thirty huddled in the compartments, vainly trying to keep warm, and were more than ready, for the food and spirits later brought by a porter and a ganger. Eventually they were to abandon the train at eleven next morning and cross the snow-covered fields to Ivybridge. Only four miles up the line was the missing 'Zulu' express, her engine buried to its smokebox in Brent station, which, after Lydford, was the most exposed on Dartmoor. (Picture, p 33). With over fifty passengers, she had left Bristol just before 6 pm in a heavy snowstorm, run through Taunton, Exeter and Newton Abbot, but towards eight o'clock halted at the top of Rattery incline to allow a train to come through the single-line Marley tunnel. For three hours she waited, her engine crew apparently seeking news of conditions down the line; at 11 pm her passengers, mostly second and third class, were roused by the crash of buffers as the 'Zulu's' guard ordered her into Brent. The station is partially sheltered by a cutting, but in a few hours the bitter cold drove everybody into the waiting-room and signal-box. Hot food and drink were scarce, and as virtually all accommodation in the village was taken up by navvies working on the new railway line, the express's complement sank wearily to the floor, shivering under rugs, coats and capes.

At dawn, a party of men defied the blizzard and got into the village, returning with a meagre supply of bloaters which, reinforced by the railwaymen's stores, were cooked over the station stove. The lot of several soldiers, sailors and marines among the passengers was pitiable. They had neither food nor money until a charitable traveller gave them a guinea, and later several Brent ladies arrived with hot dinners, drinks and tobacco for them. As the 'Zulu's' people settled down to await rescue, five miles away at Totnes there were identical scenes as the half-frozen passengers of another down express abandoned her for the station refreshment-room. This closed at 4 am and they trudged off through the snow to get what lodging they could in the town.

Every train coming behind her and the 'Zulu' was in trouble; heavy drifting on the inclines around the great Whiteball tunnel above Tiverton Junction derailed the pilot engine in front of yet another down express. A break-down crew soon arrived from Taunton, where the missing 'Flying Dutchman' with the Duke of Edinburgh on board, had been deliberately held up, but it was 6.30 am before the express, again double-headed, rolled into the junction over eight hours late. The North of England mail followed, and managed to reach Exeter some hours late, and the GWR travelling post-office got down as far as Newton Abbot.

The chaos brought by the blizzard had also struck the GWR elsewhere; the Channel Islands boat-train had nosed into a blocked cutting at Maiden Norton, and could not be freed for several hours. On Salisbury Plain, where immense drifts had built up, the main line between Salisbury and Bristol was cut at Westbury by a goods train which had set out on Monday night for Aberdare. Just outside Salisbury station another engine was derailed, adding to the confusion as it meant single-line working. A down passenger from Bristol arrived three hours late, and when the 6 am up train, which did not leave until early afternoon, became stuck, all operations were abandoned.

Two passenger trains that left Newbury for Didcot Junction had gone into drifts near Compton, and over forty passengers had to find shelter at the local inn. Heavy drifting had also temporarily paralysed the GWR in parts of South Wales; for several hours only the down rails between Pyle and Port Talbot could be worked, and a 15ft drift outside the Cynmer tunnel stopped all traffic. The line between Abergavenny and Rhymney Bridge was also blocked, and the Barry Dock Railway lost an engine for several hours in the snow. Deep snow all over the Rhondda valley stopped hundreds of miners from getting to work, besides bringing the inevitable accidents, and the furnaces of the Tredegar ironworks had to be damped down because of the blizzard and lack of workers.

The Kentish railways had also been caught on the wrong foot by the suddenness of the blizzard, and by midnight their engine crews and staff faced deep drifts on every line. On the Eltham Valley Railway, all traffic between Dover and Canterbury had ceased; the 'Tidal' train from London, due at 10.36 pm, wallowed into a cutting a mile from Newhaven, and did not arrive until 5.30 am. The last train from Charing Cross became stuck opposite Saltwood Castle, near Hythe, and did not reach Sandgate before 9 am, an hour after her famished passengers had received a makeshift breakfast from a friendly farmer. A mail train from London, which should have arrived at Portsmouth at midnight, went into a deep drift near Hilsea, and one of her carriages was derailed. Gangers who arrived in the early hours were able to release the passengers, who included Admiral Gordon and Capt Markham RN, returning from a levee.

It took considerably more effort to rescue a late night local train from Chatham which had run through Sittingbourne at 11 pm and then, as she approached Beaconhill cutting, been caught as the blizzard swept across the open marshes. In response to a telegram, a heavy goods engine was sent out from Teynham but it, too, bogged down. As dawn came, stationmaster Goymer of Faversham arrived at Teynham on a pilot engine, switched over to the down line and, aided by the goods engine, tried to push the local train through the drift. He failed, and returned to Teynham, crossed back to the up line, and vainly attempted to reach her from the other side. Eleven women were taken on board the pilot engine, but in backing clear this also became stuck. At 4 am all the local's passengers took shelter in a nearby signal-box until daylight, when a gang of 150 men from Faversham began work on the line, finally clearing it by noon.

Of all the stranded passengers some of the worst off must have been the thirty or so on board another local train on the Hythe branch of the South Eastern Railway, which left Sandby Junction just before 9 pm. A few moments later a large tree fell squarely across the mouth of the Sandby tunnel. Watchmen, alarmed by the crash, ran to a signal-box, and the local halted just in time, but was unable to go back because of drifting at the rear end of the tunnel, and she and her passengers spent the night in its dank and draughty depths.

As the bitter, murky dawn of Tuesday 10 March came, there were over a dozen complete trains marooned out in the blizzard in Devon and Cornwall alone. The GWR began rescue operations, but the engineers and gangers had to rely on shovels and the force of their engines to cut through the drifts, as all the available snowploughs, old-fashioned rams dating from 1881, were a hundred miles away at Swindon. One rescue bid had already come to nothing. The relief gang which had left Millbay at 11 pm for Horrabridge had reached Yelverton at 1 am, but it took until 10 am for the gangers to dig their way through the last four miles.

In they came [according to Mr Weekes] looking like snowmen, Father Xmas, Drowned Rats, shaking with the cold. We gave them tea and they brought with them a large basket of provisions. They drank the tea nearly boiling and declared they were so cold that it scarcely felt warm. After refreshments, off they went to get the train on the line, once more facing the storm which continued unabated. They bravely accomplished the purpose when the breakdown engine wanted water and they were obliged to leave the train and run back to the water tanks. The Horrabridge points were frozen so there was nothing for it but to go to Yelverton. Alas, outside Horrabridge was a great drift where our engines got jammed for half an hour. When free they came backwards and then gathering up steam went full speed into the snow and cut through but only to get wedged hopelessly in another, close to the water tanks at Yelverton. Here the water failed, and the engines' fires had to be put out and there they remained jammed until morning.

Singular lack of success also fell to divisional superintendent Compton, who, at 6.50 am, left North Road in a powerful pilot engine in search of the up London mail and the 'Zulu' express. Two hours later, in a blinding snowstorm he and his crew plunged into a 20ft drift on the Ivybridge end of the Bittaford viaduct. Meanwhile his assistant, superintendent Quigley, was also on the rails, heading towards Saltash. A dozen times his men dismounted to heave aside hoardings, trees and telegraph poles. High above the rooftops on Keyham viaduct they cleared more debris, and at Camel's Head hacked through the great block which had defeated Mr Compton's engine the previous evening. On reaching Saltash, Mr Quigley found the first of the missing up Cornish mail trains.

Laden with over eighty passengers, including banker Bolitho and his wife bound for the Ivybridge hunt, a honeymoon couple on their way to the Midlands, and four babies in arms, she had battled up the steep Cornish inclines and reached St Germans station, only to stop dead when the engine and carriage bogies were entangled by trailing telegraph wires. Inspector Scantlebury and fireman Gibbons pushed on through the blizzard to Saltash, continually climbing over fallen poles, and despite the gale crossed the dizzy height of the Royal Albert bridge, but soon encountered the Camel's Head block. The mail's passengers had meanwhile been evacuated to the waiting-rooms and plied with refreshments by stationmaster Priest and his staff. Hot tea and coffee was reinforced by a large tin of cream and a number of fresh eggs contributed by one of the passengers, and Mr Sara, a traveller for a chocolate firm, also willingly cut up his Easter egg samples to brew cocoa. The train was able to leave St Germans at 8 am and after another delay was met, and shepherded into Plymouth by superintendent Quigley.

Normally two hours and sixteen minutes behind her was a second up mail, due at Millbay at 10.30 pm, but she lay askew in the snow near Grampound Road station, high up on the Cornish moors. She had cleared Truro at 9.30 pm, but not until a message arrived from Grampound was it realised what had happened to her. Acting stationmaster Kately and a party went up in a relief engine, but as the red tail light of the up mail was sighted they, too, ran into a deep drift. Aided by a gang from Grampound, Mr Kately cleared his engine and, unable to go forward, returned to

Truro where news of fresh trouble awaited him. Nine wagons of a perishable goods train which had left Redruth at 10.30 pm laden with broccoli and Scilly flowers, had been derailed at Treleigh gates, just outside the town. The two goods engines were uncoupled and ran on, but the hindmost one left the rails outside Scorrier, leaving the pilot alone to steam up to Truro.

Mr Kately at once despatched a pair of engines to the scene but they could not get beyond Chacewater, and soon he and his gangs were again heading towards Grampound Road and the marooned up mail. They met her assistant guard, Hammett, a veteran of the 1881 blizzard, trudging down the line; he had already wired to Liskeard for help and then, leaving guard Kelly standing by the train, walked back to protect the rear and to discover if any assistance was on the way from Truro. Hammett gratefully climbed on board the relief engine, and they reached the mail to find a gang from Lostwithiel locomotive depot already hard at work.

Although they dug furiously around the embedded engine and coaches, it was so cold that mufflers and great-coats froze on the men's backs. Finally, at 4.30 am, the carriage was jacked back on to the rails, but it was 11 am before the mail lurched clear of the cutting, and another four hours passed before she steamed into Millbay station.

Only an hour or so before this derailment the 'Dutchman', a fast down express from Paddington to Penzance hauled by the broad-gauge 4–4–0 saddle-tank *Leopard*, had thundered through the drifts around Grampound. Only forty minutes late at Truro, she then had to wait until 9 pm for the branch train from Falmouth, which had barely managed to push through the serious blockages of trees and telegraph poles on the gradients around Perran-well. The 'Dutchman' was soon on her way, the carriages rocking and swaying as she crossed the exposed mining districts; the blizzard was at its height when she left Redruth at 10 pm, but she almost reached Camborne station before the *Leopard's* rear bogie jumped the track and the train slewed gently to a halt at Stray Park level-crossing (picture, p 85). Her guard, unsure of their whereabouts, struggled 200 yards down to the station and raised the alarm. When he returned the snow almost smothered him, but by 11 pm all the passengers were helped out of the listing carriages and taken to stationmaster Reed's house and the town's hotels.

A dozen miles away another GWR guard was having an alarming night. The evening train on the Gwinear Road—Helston branch line was over an hour late when she left the latter station at half-past seven. Driver James Cole steamed cautiously through the drifts, but a few minutes after leaving the little country station of Nancegollan the small tank engine became embedded in Polcrebbo cutting. Guard Samuel Lindsey jumped down from his van and sank neck deep in the snow, thinking for a moment that he was falling down a mineshaft. He struggled along to the footplate where driver Cole was sounding long blasts on the whistle. There followed the painfully similar scenes that were enacted on the railways throughout Devon and Cornwall that night.

Tossing aside their shovels and pinchbars, guard Lindsey, driver Cole, fireman Frank Webb and the sole passenger, farmer Matthews who was bound for Praze, the next station, settled down in the warmest compartment. By daylight, and now paralysed by the cold, they heard shouts and after scraping the ice from the windows saw two figures outside. These were two porters from Praze in search of the train, but as it was still snowing hard they climbed in as well. Around 8 am, agonisingly stiff and cold, they all set off across the fields, guard Lindsey burdened with two large bags of mail. Luckily they were close to Polcrebbo Farm and, finding a cowhouse, they crouched against the animals to warm up. Farmer Alfred

Rowe, who had been up at an early hour, was surprised by their sudden knocking on the farmhouse door, and called his wife, who cooked them a hearty breakfast. A few hours later another pair of porters arrived from Praze, one the little station boy Percy Kindrew, searching for the original pair, and at 4 pm yet two more arrived in search of the others.

Meanwhile, at Penzance, the non-appearance of the 'Dutchman' had caused a great deal of alarm, particularly as the slow train, usually fifteen minutes ahead of her, did not arrive until 11 pm. At midnight news of the derailment flashed down the wires, probably the last message to get through, and off went a breakdown train commanded by stationmaster Blair, superintendent Ivey of the locomotive department, and inspector Harris, lately known as 'Harris Pasha' because of a large woollen turban he wore throughout the blizzard. An hour later they ran into a huge drift on the gradient between Angarrack viaduct and Gwinear Road. Two more powerful engines were sent up, only to bog down in the same cutting; one drift alone was

'The gangers kept shovelling'

Page 51

(above) *Sightseers investigate a fallen tree across Athenæum Street, Plymouth;* (below) *pedestrians braving Tuesday's storm in Plymouth pass by a silent Derry's Clock, its works frozen solid*

Page 52

(above) *A snowdrift on Roborough Down, Dartmoor, some days after the blizzard;*
(below) *convicts clearing a road near Princetown, with armed prison officers in the foreground*

eighty yards long and twelve feet deep. Undeterred by the appalling cold and the snow that whirled about them, the gangers kept shovelling, and finally reached Camborne and the stranded 'Dutchman' at noon, having taken twelve hours to cover fourteen miles.

At almost the same time a well-manned breakdown train commanded by GWR inspector Northcott rolled out of Millbay to reach, if possible, Mr Compton's train at Cornwood. The relief comprised a single new carriage, double-headed by an 0–6–0 goods tank and an 0–4–0 express engine. Both were powerful enough to go up Hemerdon bank against the blizzard, but it was 3.15 pm before they reached Mr Compton, who then abandoned his train funnel-deep. The trip back was even worse, and according to John Murray, driver of the tank engine:

> We were going full speed down the incline in order to cut through the snow and when we got down to within a mile of Plympton we ran into a pile of snow seven foot high and a hundred yards long. It was too much for our engines . . . and we were fairly caught. A terrific snowstorm was then raging and we could barely see a few yards ahead. My mate and I stuck to our posts, but about an hour later I became insensible and I do not know what became of my mate . . . the snow beat in with awful force.[1]

Murray and the other driver, William Coleman, who had evidently been left behind to draw the fires of the two engines while the rest of the gang set off on foot for Plymouth, would have died but for nineteen-year-old Harold Williams and his tutor from nearby Torridge House. They found Coleman's express engine, which had become separated from the tank during the vain attempt to steam through the block, buried to its roof on the bridge which crossed the lane from the George Hotel. Coleman lay across his footplate muttering feebly 'I'm dying, I'm dying,' and after giving him brandy they carried him down the line until they encountered a rescue party of nine volunteers. They had returned to Plympton after Coleman's fireman, Samuel Moore, had caught up with the rest of the breakdown gang just as superintendent Quigley arrived on a relief engine. Coleman was borne away to Torridge House, and young Williams and his tutor later brought in Murray. It took three hours to revive him, and it was some time before it was certain that he would live.

Back at Millbay the platforms were crowded with would-be passengers and people seeking news of relatives, but as every telegraph line was down, there was little the stationmaster could tell them. The arrival of the up Cornish mails, one ten hours late and the other sixteen, and the departure of the various breakdown trains, had created momentary excitement, but this soon dissolved, and as the cold and miserable day wore on there was 'no incident to vary the monotony of the day, except the occasional fall of panes of glass from the roof on to the platform, occasioned by the weight of snow above.'[2]

Up at Horrabridge station the saga of the 6.10 pm from Launceston continued, and Mr Weekes became grimly reconciled to a second night in his uncomfortable situation.

The two ladies were taken down to a cottage to sleep but those of us that remained in the station had a worse night of it for in came a dozen or so of the breakdown gang all drenching with snow and ice and began carousing and shouting but after a while fought their way to the Public House nearby for a 'quiet half-hour'. We shall have a time of it when they come back, we thought but were greatly surprised for they came back worn out with the toils of the day, lay on the floor and were asleep in five minutes, and we nodded in our hard wooden chairs but thought that our own arms and legs went to sleep more than our brains.

Such was Monday night on the railways and Tuesday's

aftermath, yet one more train was still to come to grief in the snow. Mr Kately's gangs, which had helped to rescue the up mail at Grampound, had gone with her as far as Par, where they encountered a down passenger from Millbay. They retraced their steps with her to Truro and at 4 pm she left on the return journey to Plymouth with a few passengers and two vans of meat. The unabated blizzard caught her in a deep cutting near St Blazey; under-guard William Westaway stayed by the train while his assistant Henry Johnson walked back to St Austell. He returned with signalman Bailey and supplies for the engine crew, but already five passengers including a Par woman, led by a man from Bodmin who knew the way, had abandoned the train. Making 'a bridge with foot-warmers' they crossed the drift between the carriage and the cutting side, scaled the fence and set off across the meadows. They reached the high road to find it blocked, and only by walking on the hedgetops did they reach Par, completely exhausted, at dawn.

4

Monday night on the Channel shore

Mrs Briggs, horrified by what she had seen from the upstairs window, hurried down to find head keeper Jones. He sent off a mounted messenger to warn chief officer Crickett of Hallsands coastguards, who realised that the ship in distress was the big steamer last sighted off the Skerries bank. The nearest lifeboat, at Salcombe, faced an impossible four-mile pull against the gale; indeed the local packet steamers *Express* and *Kingsbridge Packet* had barely cleared Salcombe bar at dusk on their return to Plymouth, arriving after 'a fearfully rough passage, scarce being able to see anything for the blinding snow storm'.

A glance along the surf-swept northern shore of Start Bay told Mr Crickett that neither would the Dartmouth lifeboat put to sea that evening. As the nearest rocket gear was at Rickham, near Salcombe, he ordered a horseman to fetch the Prawle Point coastguards, who would bring this with them. Another galloped off to alert chief officer Ridge at Torcross, two miles along Start Bay. Crickett then led his men down to the cliffs.

The easterly gale was still rising, and keeper Jones confirmed that there was no sign of survivors or wreckage. An hour passed before a faint blue light appeared far out in the gloom, but reluctant to keep his weary men searching in such weather Crickett sent one man to investigate and led the rest back to Hallsands, on the way rescuing from a drift one Harvey, an army pensioner. Hardly was the old man set before the fire than at 8.30 pm distress rockets went up almost halfway to Torcross. Floundering thigh-deep in snow the coastguards reached Beesands village to find ashore the 173-ton schooner *Lunesdale* of Barrow, London to Runcorn with whitening, which had been running blindly before the storm since passing the Isle of Wight at 11 am. Torcross coastguards had so far failed to reach her, but a fisherman named Roper dashed out into the sea and hurled a line to Capt William Jones, who leapt from the mizzen lee rigging and was saved by Ridge and others wading chest deep. The rest of the *Lunesdale's* crew, also clinging to the rigging, were washed away and drowned.

The Prawle coastguards and rocket men did not arrive until 10 pm, too late to help in the rescue. So, by an unlucky chance, all the Start coastguards were at Beesands when the 73-ton Chester schooner *Lizzie Ellen*, Robert Dodd master, from Charlestown to London with china clay but beaten back from Portland Bill, broached-to under Hallsands cliff. Six fishermen, George Stone, Thomas and Robert Trout, James Lynn, William Mitchell and John Patey, rescued mate James Smith and Bob Clemens, a Plymouth sailor, by rope, but the schooner's boy, Francis Davies, refused to jump overboard. Unable to persuade him, Capt Dodd himself was swept away and drowned, and soon afterwards the boy, crying piteously for his mother, also vanished. The ship's dog was saved, but the schooner went to pieces.

Ninety miles up Channel the blizzard was howling across the great promontory of Dungeness, and the Kentish coastguards were called to action at an early hour. Shortly after 7.30 pm the 99-ton Fleetwood schooner *Hugh Barclay*, stone-laden from Guernsey to London, drove ashore from the exposed eastern roadstead. She struck far out on the shelving sands, and the coastguards were still trying to reach her an hour later when the 170-ton schooner *Echo* of Llanelly grounded on the sand opposite the Great Stone.

The Lydd lifeboat was crewed mostly by coastguards, and though 'the seas were running mountains high . . . nothing daunted, the men manned the boat and she was launched in a terrific sea with the greatest possible difficulty.'[1] One lifeboatman was instantly flung overboard, but was hauled back; another breaker roared in, and the lifeboat herself went right over. Buoyed up by their cork jackets, the men clambered back on board, and pulled for the *Echo*, but the boat capsized again and moments later struck heavily on Faggot groyne and drove into the shallows. All her crew crawled ashore in a tangle of broken oars, lines and debris, but three of them, chief boatman Thomas Sullivan, who had taken the place of another man, chief boatman Hunt, and coastguard William Ryan, aged thirty-seven, a native of Helston in Cornwall, later died of exposure and injuries.

Meanwhile the 681-ton Norwegian barque *Allette* of Drammen, bound from the Baltic to Liverpool with deals and flooring boards, drove into the surf opposite No 1 coastguard station at Littlestone. Capt Olaf Gullichen and his twelve crew leapt ashore and soon afterwards the *Allette* caught fire when the galley stove capsized, 'the flames ascending high into the air and lighting up the country for miles around'. She was still burning when the Clyde steamer passed up Channel forty-eight hours later.

By 10.30 pm the tide had ebbed sufficiently for the coast-guards to reach the schooner *Hugh Barclay*, though three rockets were fired before a line fell on board, and one of the two sailors landed died on the beach. Capt Charles Bennett and the mate had already been plucked from the rigging by the waves.

Theirs were not the only lives lost that night on the storm-lashed coasts of Kent and Sussex. John Brands, engineer of the London tug *Bulldog*, came ashore to telegraph her owners from New Romney, but could not re-embark and wandered around the dunes until he collapsed and froze to death. A dozen miles away the Deal coastguards and pilots heard the faint thud of distress rockets far out on the Goodwins, and so perished Capt Couch of Fowey and the four crew of the 127-ton Brixham brigantine *Zingra*, a fortnight out from Antwerp to London with phosphates. Another vessel was in serious difficulties eight miles ENE of the North Goodwin lightship. She was the London schooner *Scout*, also out of Antwerp with phosphates, which had her bows smashed by a barque that loomed out of the driving snow, but was able to reach Newhaven, decks awash.

The suddenness of the blizzard had also caught the fishing fleet of Hastings, which had put out on Sunday afternoon, and as darkness fell the eastern shore was lined by families awaiting their return. The lights of the approaching luggers could be glimpsed among the wave-crests, but they could not beach at their usual spot eastward of the fish market. One lugger came in at Breed's slipway, some at the Queen's Hotel slip, and others as far to leeward as Bo-peep.

Anxiety increased among the waiting families as the boats ran through the surf, though horses, men and ropes were ready for them. The first lugger to fall before the storm was the *William*, William 'Hard Times' Fullgar owner and master, which at 8.30 pm struck Shelter Rocks at the end of All Saints' Street. Heavily damaged, she was tossed right over the rocks, but her crew scrambled to safety. A quarter of an hour later the 5-ton *Linnet*, Richard Gallop owner and master, ran on to the rocks directly opposite the eastern end of the Marine Parade. Even as coastguards and fishermen raced across the beach or leapt from rock to rock towards her, the 10-year-old *Linnet* went to pieces. All but twenty-two-year-old Henry Adams escaped, and he would have been saved had not coastguard Talbot jammed his leg in a crevice just as he was about to grab the young fisherman.

Within the hour word came that the eighteen-year-old lugger *Henrietta*, Charles 'Scotchie' Phillips master, had struck athwart a groyne at Bo-peep and broken up. Phillips and Henry 'Tring' Brazier, whose father and brother had been lost in a Hastings lugger off Dymchurch Wall years before, were drowned, but George 'Duke' Phillips crawled ashore and reached a cottage near St Leonard's. The two dead fishermen were later washed up near Bexhill; and the bitter snowswept dawn also revealed the foremast of the wrecked *Linnet* floating off the Albion Hotel at Hastings. On the beach lay her keel and some pathetic debris: a stove, ropes, planks, a fog bell, and the body of young Adams, his arms raised in the act of hauling off his Guernsey frock. The seas had gone down, but the Hastings fleet had suffered cruelly. The luggers *Mayflower*, *John and James*, and *Shah*, lay battered beyond repair, and the *Lady Brassey* and the *Lois* were just hulks, while the whole shore was covered with wreckage of every description.

The packet *Victoria*, which had sailed from Dover regardless of the weather and without her distinguished passenger, the Duchess of Edinburgh, had run into the full force of the blizzard. She made little headway and 'the waves seemed to threaten to crush the sides of the steamer, and the wind scooped the water out of the Channel and dashed it into sheets of spray, which swept the decks with unrestrained fury'.[2] Capt Shirley and his officers soon lost their reckoning and at 10.30 pm, having just sounded ten fathoms, they had reduced speed in the belief that they were approaching Cap Gris Nez when the *Victoria* grounded on a sandy bottom. A tremendous squall then swept the ship and she washed clear of the shoal. At 2 am Capt Shirley hove-to, and soon after that the packet was pooped by an enormous sea which swept her decks, flattened the guard rails and poured down into the cabins. She anchored until 4 am, when Calais harbour was sighted in a lull in the snow, but she did not get in until after 9 am, so short of bunker coal that another hour at sea would have left her helpless with dead engines. Even now the ordeal of her passengers, who had spent the night in the saloon huddled in rugs, blankets and tablecloths, was not over. Rope after rope parted as quaymen and the packet's crew tried to get her alongside, and twice it was feared she would be driven ashore. At last, after smashing a lifeboat on the Ostend staging, the *Victoria* was berthed, her dishevelled passengers hurriedly disembarked and Capt Shirley left again to seek shelter farther down the coast.

Other mail packets like the *Victoria* were out in the blizzard. The Ostend steamer did not reach Dover until 10 am, just as the French mailboat sailed, both being ten hours late. Another Ostend steamer which left soon after 6 am had to be towed back, and the mail steamer *Maid of Kent* arrived from Calais early in the afternoon, having taken fifteen hours to get across against tremendous seas, which had also forced the government cable ship *Monarch*, engaged in laying the London to Paris telephone cable, to abandon her task and heave-to in the Downs. None of the packets had been seriously harmed, but the small steam coaster *Neptune*, which had sailed from Guernsey only hours before the blizzard broke, almost sank in heavy seas. Twice she was pooped, and Capt Eastwood and mate Green were hurled overboard. Eventually, with fires out, decks swept and heavily damaged, she was towed into Portland by the steamer *Headworth*.

Due to the disruption of all communications, news of the disasters at Start Point did not penetrate inland, but even if it had the authorities at Plymouth already had enough to contend with. By seven in the evening the busy streets of the 'three towns', Plymouth, Devonport and Stonehouse, were almost empty. Great snowfilled gusts roared in from the Sound, and shop, house, villa and tenement shuddered under the blast. Slates, tiles, gutterings and balustrades crashed on to the pavements, and hoardings and signs were hurled far and wide. The trams retreated to their Mutley depot, though not before No 9 was nearly wrecked when a hoarding fell squarely in front of the horses on the way down Devonport Hill. Even the cabmen, perhaps the hardiest individuals of the age, gave up and took their shivering horses home. Early casualties were the tall elms and poplars which rose from the shrubberies about many villas. Down they came by the score, one filled Buckland Street from gutter to gutter, and another, falling in Athenæum Gardens, blocked the main approach to North Road station, but luckily nobody was hurt by any of them.

Around eight o'clock, with the gale blowing a hurricane from ENE, the rain of debris was punctuated by the fall of heavier brickwork and masonry. In Clifton Place, Devonport, three small girls escaped injury when a chimney crashed through the roof of their bedroom; rubble blocked the stairs, and they were rescued by ladder. Children of the tobacconist next door to the Devonport post office also emerged unharmed from the wreckage surrounding their beds.

As violent squalls continued thundering over the city, the damage increased. Soldiers on duty at the guardhouse of Raglan Barracks, high up on Devonport Hill, ducked as their windows shattered in a heavy gust, and the roof of the 'Crown and Column' public house and an adjacent off-licence began shedding slates and laths in all directions. Down in Albert Road an ex-bluejacket named Pyle went up to a back bedroom to nail up a board to stop the fire smoking. Suddenly the house shook, there was a tremendous crash, and he found himself sitting before the living-room fire, surrounded by his fallen chimney. Another naval man, stoker Jones of HMS *Aurora*, his wife and mother-in-law, were almost buried when a brickwork stack demolished most of the roof of their Cannon Street home.

The storm and flying debris did not prevent one act of extreme courage that evening. Messrs Harris Bros, painters and decorators, were engaged in painting a large furniture warehouse, and as the gale increased it was feared their ladders would come down. One of their workmen, named Bode, volunteered to secure them; up he went, sixty feet above the pavement, and roped the ladders to the gutterings. Hardly had he come down when a large plate glass window in the warehouse was blown in and had to be boarded up.

One of the luckiest escapes was that of the family of Mr Perkins, surveyor to Lord Edgcumbe, at Emma Place, Stonehouse. His wife had just gone up to fasten the nursery shutters when the quiet order of a Victorian household disintegrated with a roar as a massive chimney stack plummeted through the roof. Mrs Perkins, standing by the fireplace, recovered to find herself perched on a few broken boards, all that remained of the floor. Opposite her the maid clung to the window frame and below them gaped the shattered living-room. Mr Perkins rescued them by ladder, and was then horrified to find that he had propped it on some debris which could easily have slipped and tumbled them all into the basement.

Another large brickwork chimney collapsed at 4 Wingfield Terrace, Stoke, seconds after the nurse had carried the youngest daughter of Mr Venning, town clerk of Devonport, from the nursery. The nursery fire spilled through the broken floor into the living-room and ignited oil from an upset lamp. Immediately the ornate furnishings caught alight, and as Wingfield Terrace stood on a hill exposed to the storm, the flames soon became an inferno.

'Devonport fire brigade galloped up'

Bells clanging, the Devonport fire brigade galloped up, having been delayed by the slippery streets. When they failed to save the villa's interior, they turned their hoses on the roof. Soon they were reinforced by the Stonehouse brigade, who, unable to find any hydrants, joined in the salvage of Mr Venning's property. Already busy on this dangerous job were a large body of police and a party of soldiers and marines from Raglan Barracks, commanded by Capt Liardet, RMLI, and Capt Andrew Haggard, KOSB, brother of the famous author. The flames suddenly roared higher, and they retreated as the roof fell in, almost on top of Capt Goodeve, RN, officer of the day, who was trying to throw a chest of silver plate from an upper window. It was later found melted into a single lump.

The villa next door, home of the widow of Admiral How, was in serious danger, but the West of England fire brigade arrived and, though hampered by low water pressure, got the blaze under control by breaking open a ceiling and playing their hoses on the rafters. So great was the heat from No 4 that No 2, owned by the Rev St Aubyn, rector of Stoke Damerell, was also threatened. His staff hurriedly piled furniture and belongings alongside the growing heap in the road outside, and, just as the danger of fire passed, the end chimney stack suddenly swayed and fell straight through the roof, demolishing everything in its path.

By ten o'clock the fire was almost out, and the inevitable crowd of spectators drifted away. At Millbridge, the hurricane blew them hither and thither towards the seething waters of the Deadlake (filled and known since 1904 as Victoria Park). Panic ensued as those in front tried to come back, and those behind sought to go forward; eventually most people went home via Pennycomequick and North Road, though this was almost as bad as the blizzard swept down the valley.

Up on Plymouth Hoe the stalwart snow-encrusted statue of Sir Francis Drake stood firm amongst a riot of uprooted bushes, broken glass, smashed fencing and overturned summer seats. The Sound, though sheltered by the eastern land of Staten Heights and the great breakwater, was filled with high and breaking seas. By nine o'clock every vessel in Sutton harbour was dragging, and all the east coast trawlers struck their topmasts and broke out extra warps. No craft dared venture to the mouth of Millbay docks, and a few hundred yards to leeward around Devil's Point, buoys, yachts and lighters rolled wildly as heavy seas surged into the mouth of the Tamar.

Blue flares went up off Torpoint, and there was a rumour that the old wooden-walled training ships *Lion* and *Im-*

placable had grounded off Thanckness, where a nasty sea was rolling over the mudflats. Every spare tug came down-river ready to rescue the hundreds of boys on board, but it was a false alarm. They had been moored stern to stern as usual in the Hamoaze, when the 3,222-ton *Implacable* parted her starboard bridle and sheared the covered gangway connecting her to the *Lion*, and both had then dragged slightly in a violent gust. While the tugs hooted and fussed about the two hulks, another was busy saving the Queen's Harbourmaster's cutter, which was crippled by heavy seas off Devil's Point. Her five crew were landed, but at midnight the brand new 15-ton coastguard tender *Julia*, lying unmanned inside Drake's Island, parted her anchor cable and drove on to Bottlenose Point near Millbay dock.

Out on the exposed waters of the Sound, more naval ships were tearing at their moorings. Another boys' training hulk, the 3,880-ton *Impregnable*, the gunnery school ship *Cambridge* and the armourclad broadsider *Achilles* inched closer to Drake's Island. Defying the hurricane, tugs and lighters steamed out of Devonport and, under Commander Burniston, had by dawn transferred fresh anchors and hawsers to the imperilled warships.

Down in Cawsand Bay, which was just too far to leeward of the breakwater to be sheltered in an easterly gale, there was havoc. Ten fishing hookers broke up or sank at their moorings, and the unmanned 31-ton pilot cutter *Mystery*, John Hooper master and owner, drove into a small cove under the coastguard station on Redding Point. In the village one cottage had its slate-hung front stripped bare, and the wall of a house being built opposite Willcox's inn was blown bodily into the bar. The roads from Cremyll and Millbrook were blocked before midnight, and every late traveller was forced to unharness and lead his horse across the military camp through 4ft snowdrifts to reach Cawsand and Kingsand.

Sixty miles down Channel Falmouth was, if anything, in greater chaos, as its waterfront took the brunt of the storm. Pendennis Point usually kept the worst of an easterly gale from the inner harbour, but tonight heavy seas were rolling into even the quietest backwater and creek. One side of the town's main street backs on to the harbour, and during the 'nineties grocers, tailors, tobacconists, roperies and laundries stood side by side, ready to supply the windjammers and steamers which arrived every day, and these were the buildings which took the hammer-blows of the easterly hurricane. As in Plymouth, slates, gutterings and chimney stacks were falling by mid-evening, and an early casualty was the front window of the famous 'Old Curiosity Shop'. Two policemen, among the few people still tramping the snow, helped the celebrated Edward Burton to board up his window, and he was then appalled to find that a slate had hurtled between a pair of eighty-guinea vases. A few hundred yards away on the 'Moor', Falmouth's main square, a cheapjack from Redruth struggled to keep his tent up in the gale. The storm won, and he retreated to a nearby inn, leaving his goods rapidly vanishing under the snow.

At eight o'clock the lifeboat maroons sounded from the docks, but the *Bob Newbons* and her tug could not put out, and nobody knew where the distressed ship lay. Down in the harbour heavy seas played havoc; a large sailing punt owned by Neville Tuke, the marine artist, drove into a small dock formed by Market Strand quay and a fishyard owned by a Mrs Downing, and was broken up by the coal hulk *Reform*, which wallowed out of the darkness on top of her. Pounding against the dock wall like a 200-ton battering ram, the hulk stove in the back of a fishermen's rest, recoiled, and demolished Mrs Downing's back wall, before coming to rest with its counter overhanging the yard.

The noise of rending timber and falling masonry brought sailors and boatmen running, but they were powerless in the turmoil, even when the 60-ton trawling ketch *Kingston* cannoned into the *Reform* and rolled over on to the mud. Some 300 yards away, at Fishstrand pier, a quay punt was hurled under the fish stores owned by the Chard family. Soon afterwards, Mr Chard's own cutter, the *Queen*, stove-in her stern, and his crab pots, luckily emptied that afternoon, sank beneath the waves. Further along between the now demolished gasworks and Custom House quay, Fox's sampling gig capsized, and Lean's cutter *Ada* stranded, but boatmen managed to work her into a quiet corner.

To add to the general noise and confusion, the galvanised roof of Lean's store, where the schooner *Mary Barrow* lay on the building stocks, and that of the Falmouth Trading Co went whirling over the town. A stone wall behind a jeweller's shop suddenly slid into the river, then the whole rear of the shop followed, and a neighbouring photographic studio lost its roof. Up in the town the Porthcawl Coal Co's store was also stripped to bare rafters, and the occasional pedestrian dodged for cover from flying slates and some of the tall elms in Arwenack Street, which brought telegraph wires and poles down with them.

As the evening wore on the devastation in the harbour increased, and many ships were blown upriver towards Penryn and Greenbank. The Falmouth Coal Co's tug *Carbon* sank at anchor; the Harbour Board's tug *Arwenack* collided with the lugger *Dove*, which also broke loose and wrecked herself in Harvey's Dock. The runaway *Arwenack* was boarded by Maunder, her chief engineer, with the boatmen Hingston and Jose, who dropped anchor only yards from the rocks. Another tug, the brand-new *Hercules*, owned by Cox & Co, came flying up Penryn creek and slewed broadside on the mud off the granite works. A few hundred yards away Rusden's cutter *Norma* crashed into Greenbank cliff, while the tug *Victor*, bows telescoped by collision with a dredger, grounded close by.

Amid the chaos blue lights went up off Trefusis Point, where the Padstow schooner *Annie*, arsenic-laden from Restronguet to Swansea, had broken adrift and fouled the jibboom of a three-masted schooner. Her mainmast came down, but the tug *Triton* put a hawser on board, the *Annie's* anchors were slipped, and both craft ran up to Penryn. Out in Carrick Roads more blue flares were burning, and within an hour the tug *Briton* had hauled the brig *Blanche*, Owen master, of and from Yarmouth to Cardiff with flour, clear of the wave-swept eastern breakwater. Across the water at St Mawes the Coverack Stone Co's 30-ton steam barge *Helen* sheared her cables in a strong gust and drove under St Mawes castle, but luckily she was unmanned. Other sailing barges were scattered all over the creek, and one smashed into pilot cutter No 8, both being nearly wrecked by the collision.

A few miles up the coast, at the fishing village of Portscatho, huge seas had already destroyed part of the quay, flattened the coastguard watch-hut, and gutted their boathouse. They were still gathering up the pieces when, at 6.30 pm, the 566-ton iron screw schooner-rigged steamer *Dundela* of Belfast, twelve days out from the Azores to London with a part cargo of forty tons of oranges and pineapples, ran on to the Straythe rocks, four miles up the coast near Portloe. She had burned so much bunker coal steaming up from Ushant against the gale that Capt Reid bore up for Dartmouth, but subsequently altered course for Falmouth and, at 4 pm, fell in behind a barque going down Channel. For two hours the *Dundela*, riding high and light, floundered to leeward until, deep in Veryan Bay, she refused to answer her helm and drifted ashore.

Capt Reid saw the coastguards' flares telling that rescue was at hand, and ordered everybody to stay on board. Several of the crew, over-anxious for their safety, defied orders, and Charlie Taylor, the young messroom boy, was lowered over the side. Suddenly he shrieked 'Haul me up!'

but the rope went slack and they saw him standing on the rocks, having slipped out of the bowline. As he tried to get ashore a breaker swirled around the *Dundela's* bows and swept him away. After waiting some time for a rocket line, Capt Reid gave the order to abandon ship, and aided by deep-sea lead lines his crew leapt on to the rocks, not yet realising quite how close they were to the cliffs. The captain slipped and hung by his finger-tips until second officer Edwards dragged him back. They came off last, supporting chief officer Kirsten, whose hands had been badly burned when he thrust the wrong end of a distress rocket into the galley stove.

Meanwhile the mounted messenger sent to fetch Portscatho rocket brigade had taken a long time to reach his destination through the snow-filled lanes, and it was midnight before chief officer Pope and his men set off for Portloe. There followed 'a fearful march with four horses' through snow so deep that in places it rose shoulder high to the animals. They found the *Dundela's* crew in front of roaring cottage fires, and there was nothing to do but begin the long trek home. As they climbed the steep hill out of the little village another steamer began burning flares out in Veryan Bay, and despite warning rockets the 930-ton *Carl Hirschberg*, Malhouse master, of and from Hamburg in water ballast for Cardiff, lurched ashore in the lee of the Flagstaff, right outside Portloe Cove. Capt Malhouse at first declined to abandon ship as the seas had lessened with the ebb tide, and there was still plenty of water under his keel. While he tried to back clear, a lifeboat containing two sailors shot out from the steamer's lee and capsized off the rocks. Chief boatman Ivey of the coastguard seized a lifeline and, aided by several fishermen, rescued one man; the other received a hard buffeting before he was hauled out by farmer John Blamey, who had been the first man to reach the *Dundela*. Soon afterwards, the rest of the Germans came ashore, and the *Carl Hirschberg* was left ebbing dry in a lagoon, sheltered from the worst of the seas. (Picture, p 104.)

Back on the cliffs at Start Point, events had taken a serious turn for the second time that night. Just before midnight head lightkeeper Jones, standing in the yard of his home, saw a ship's navigation lights beneath the northern and steepest side of the headland. He and his keepers, clutching each other to keep upright, went down the steep slope to the cliff edge. A hundred feet below them the waves broke in a cataract of spray, but there was no trace of a vessel. Chief officer Crickett and his men, wading home to Hallsands, also saw what they believed to be a steamer's lights. They fired a rocket and burned blue flares, but a few minutes later the lights vanished.

This fresh activity also brought chief officer Ridge and the Torcross coastguards down to the Start, where they encountered the lightkeepers, who told them of the supposed wreck. Mr Ridge had already taken the precaution of sending a horseman after chief officer Hewitt and his men, who were returning to Prawle. They were intercepted at Chivelstone Cross and wearily retraced their steps through the snow and over fallen trees. It was 2 am before they reached the Start and joined the other coastguards, whose eyes, through staring seawards, 'seemed as if they were being pricked with needles', and were to remain bloodshot for several days.

Meanwhile a drenched and barefoot sailor had staggered to the cottage of William Partridge near Prawle Point and, though almost speechless with cold, identified himself in broken English to Lloyd's signalman John Perry and coastguard Rich as John Nielsen, a Swedish fireman. He also intimated that there were other survivors, but a search by Perry and Rich revealed no trace of them, until on a fresh sweep of the cliffs, aided by two other coastguards, they found two more Swedish stokers under a furze break just beyond Langstone Point. While Perry led them back to

Prawle, coastguards Shelbourne and Smythe tried without success to revive a third sailor lying in a drift.

The Swedes were the only survivors from the steamer Mrs Briggs saw, the 2,177-ton iron screw schooner-rigged *Marana*, owned by George Bell & Co of Liverpool, which had sailed from Victoria Docks at 11 am on Sunday for Colombo, via Cardiff for bunkers, with a cargo of 2,000 wooden railway sleepers and telegraph poles.

The blizzard caught her in the Downs, and at 3 pm chief officer Edward Browning stowed the auxiliary sail, though speed was kept up until two hours later, when the fore lookouts raised a cry of 'Land right ahead!' The *Marana* struck violently by the bows; Nielsen leapt from his bunk and ran on deck just as the steamer swung broadside to the Blackstone reef and her propellor and rudder carried away. In the engine-room Anders Johannsen, another survivor who had lodgings next door to Nielsen in Whitechapel, had been hurled off his feet by the tremendous impact, and when chief engineer Winter ordered him topsides he, too, was surprised to see the Start light flashing through the snow. He went to fetch his warm jacket, and so was the only man who failed to get a lifebelt, but Capt Frigginson took pity on the elderly Swede, who had been twelve years in the British Merchant Marine, and handed him his own. As the port lifeboat was jammed by the ship's list, twenty-two men, including the Swedes, crowded into the starboard boat, while the captain, officers and the messroom steward lowered the jollyboat. A violent snow squall then swept down, but not before they saw their steamer break up and sink, still flying the distress pennant at her yard-arm. The boats soon lost touch, and after failing to land in Lannacombe Bay the lifeboat twice capsized in heavy seas before breaking up on the 'Mag' ledge in Horsley cove, leaving the Swedes alone to reach the clifftops.

As dawn broke, a mere greying of the driving snow and flying spray, the coastguards, who had been on duty for almost fourteen hours, saw a ship's bows jutting from among the masses of wreckage where the mysterious lights had been sighted at midnight. Coastguard Polyblank soon discovered a sailor clinging to a slanting rock known as 'John Hatherly's Nose'. He was barely conscious and unable to retrieve a line, so keeper Briggs gallantly went down the cliff on a rope, but as he made for the rock the sailor suddenly lost hold and somersaulted into the waves.

Who he was and from whence he came was never discovered, but the broken bows belonged to the 1,039-ton iron barque *Dryad*, of Liverpool, William Thomas of Treville master, six days out from Newcastle, bound around the Horn for Valparaiso with coal, coke and mining machinery. All her twenty-six crew, which included a Cornish chief officer, J. E. Glanville of Fowey, had perished when she sailed into the cliffs between midnight and 1 am.

Her wreck was to remain unidentified for another day, and news of the Start disasters did not reach Liverpool for another forty-eight hours, after a telegram was sent out on a train from Kingswear to Exeter. On Thursday 12 March the *Liverpool Echo* carried the headlines 'Terrible Shipwrecks. Two Disasters on the South Coast. Over 40 Lives Lost'. The second wreck did not refer to the *Dryad*, but to one of the most agonising disasters on the Cornish coast, which happened only an hour after that barque struck the Start cliffs.

5

Tuesday morning at Nare Head

As evening drew into night, a tall ship was thrashing her way through the wind and snow, somewhere off the Lizard. She was the four-masted full-rigger *Bay of Panama*, pride of James Bullock's Bay line of Bengal clippers. But for the weather she would have discharged and paid off alongside the Dundee jute wharves two weeks before, and little did Capt David Wright, his wife and crew realise that during the next twenty hours they and their handsome ship would pass for ever into the legends of the great March blizzard.

The *Bay of Panama* began her career as Yard No 164 at Harland & Wolff's of Belfast, where her long steel hull first touched water on 17 October 1883. She was the fifth and last of the 'Bay' clippers, and all were renowned for their looks and speed, even at a time when every other barque or full-rigger was a 'flyer'. The *Bay of Bengal*, a

1,527-ton iron ship, was considered a masterpiece of sail when launched by John Elder of Govan in 1875. Her equally graceful sister, the 1,554-ton iron ship *Bay of Biscay*, left the same yard only a few months later, and in September that year Alexander Hall of Aberdeen launched the *Bay of Naples*, another beautifully proportioned iron clipper, of 1,621 tons. In 1878 they were joined by the *Bay of Cadiz*, a superb steel full-rigger of 1,626 tons, built by J. & G. Thompson on the Clyde.

But in size and looks the *Bay of Panama* eclipsed all her sisters, and was held by many seamen to be the finest full-rigged four-masted ship ever built. She was launched at a time when the square-riggers had begun to feel seriously the encroachment of the despised 'steamboat', whose stumpy masts and belching funnels were nudging their yard-arms in every port from Melbourne to Valparaiso. Sail had been largely ousted from the wool and emigrant runs, and even the China tea trade was being monopolised by steam. In reply to this competition came the great clippers of the 'seventies, and the 'carriers' of the 'eighties and early 'nineties; heavily-sparred barques and ships whose long, wall-sided hulls were capable of swallowing several thousand tons of coal, wheat or nitrate, and carrying them at a cost which was considerably less than for a comparable size of steamer, half filled with bunkers and engine-room.

The *Bay of Panama* was a carrier and she was big; her gross tonnage was 2,365, register 2,281 tons and deadweight 3,525 tons. Light, she displaced 1,580 tons, and laden, 5,105 tons, drawing 21ft 7in aft. From the tip of her spike bowsprit, a design which had just become fashionable, to the strake of her whalebacked poop, she measured 340ft; this was 30ft longer than the *Bay of Cadiz*, and 130ft longer than the immortal *Cutty Sark*. With a beam of 42ft and a depth of 24ft 6in, she utterly dwarfed the famous tea clipper. From deck to truck the fore, main and mizzen masts towered 140ft, almost the height of Nelson's Column, while the jigger mast soared 110ft above the helmsman's head. Each was square-rigged, carrying topgallants, topsails and royals, with a spanker and gaff spanker on the jigger. The yards were just as massive; the main yard 2ft thick and 84ft long, the topsail yard 68ft long, and the highest, the royal 46ft. When all sail, including jibs and staysails, were set, 38,528sq yd, approximately 8 acres, of best Baltic flax canvas took the wind, which, under favourable conditions, could drive the *Bay of Panama* through the seas at 10 or 12 knots.

This was the ship that hoisted the Bullock houseflag for the first time in Belfast Lough on 12 January 1884, but notwithstanding their elegance, none of the Bay line was long-lived. The *Bay of Biscay* was by then already gone, lost in a South Atlantic gale in February 1880. The South Pacific claimed the *Bay of Cadiz* in April 1889 after she had left Newcastle, New South Wales, for San Francisco with coal, and a decade later the *Bay of Naples* was posted missing while under the Russian flag. The last to go was the oldest; the *Bay of Bengal*, lost with all hands off the Tuskar rock while bound from Cardiff to Chile in March 1905. Not one man survived from four of the sisters; but the most macabre fate of all was reserved for the fifth and greatest of the ill-starred line.

The *Bay of Panama* had spent her life in the Calcutta jute trade, not surprisingly as James Bullock had considerable interests in India. His brother John operated the big iron ship *Glenroy*, the barque *Nighthawk* and the steamer *Mary Theresa*; an associate company ran two more sailing ships and a small steamer, besides which the brothers acted as Lloyd's agents at Chittagong and the Burmese rice ports of Akyab, Bassein and Moulmein. The *Bay of Panama's* towering masts and long black hull, which never carried the traditional painted ports or elegant figurehead, became a familiar sight among the tiers of ships moored fore and aft in the swiftly flowing Hooghli, awnings rigged and, in the cyclone season when tidal bores surged upriver, top-gallant yards struck and jibbooms hove in.

Calcutta, though ninety miles from the sea, was the centre of the thriving jute trade which by the eighties had become the refuge of many square-riggers pushed off their normal runs by the hated steamers. Among the 'Bay' clippers' companions moored off Garden Reach, Princept Ghat, or the Esplanade, were such famous names as *Rhoderick Dhu*, *McCullum More* and *Thomasina McClellan*, as well as 'Abbeys', 'Falls', 'Monarchs', and the Corry line's 'Stars'; at one time or another almost every British windjammer was in the jute trade. Cargoes out were usually Cheshire salt from Liverpool, Welsh or Lancashire coal for the Indian railways or steamer coaling stations, case oil from the Texan Gulf ports, and occasional loads of railway iron, cement or telegraph poles. Once discharged, and providing a suitable freight was secured (and sometimes a ship might wait several months for a cargo home), the big square bales of jute, each weighing about 3cwt dry, were loaded on board. Apart from the government salt dock and the pontoons at Budge Budge where oil was always discharged, there were no docks on the Hooghli, and the jute was ferried out by lighters and barges and swung on board by derricks. It was then jammed down into a solid mass by gangs of sweating coolies using hand-operated screwjacks.

Ashore in the groggeries and beer-halls along Flag Street, Ballasteer Road and the Kiddipore coal dock, the crews drank, fought and rioted: seamen from the Hamburg and Bremen clippers, who congregated at the notorious den known as the 'German Barracks', Dutch packet men, hard-bitten Yankees from the case oilers, and the variegated crews of the British coolie ships. Cholera was endemic, and the Hooghli full of floating corpses; every morning it was the duty of the apprentices to fend them off the moorings and gangways.

This was the world that the *Bay of Panama* left for the

'Down the Hooghli in tow of the Clive Company's paddle tug'

last time on 18 November 1890, laden with 1,784 bales of jute for Dundee, and homeward bound for England for the first time in two years. She went down the Hooghli in tow of the usual Clive Company's paddle tug, and twenty hours later brought up off Sandheads, where the regal figure of the Bengal pilot accompanied by his punkah wallah returned to the natty white-ported brig hovering in the distance. On board the clipper were thirty-six souls; Capt David Wright of Liverpool; his wife; chief officer Bullock of Birmingham; second officer Allnut of Hull; four apprentices, Beresford, Forbes, Allport and Ingliss; an Irish carpenter, Scottish sailmaker, Yankee bosun, Welsh bosun's mate, four quartermasters, cook, steward, and eighteen able and ordinary seamen, the usual mixture of English, Welsh, Irish and Scandinavians. The *Bay of Panama's* was a crack crew.

The voyage home around the Cape of Good Hope was uneventful and comparatively slow. Most jute ships averaged eighty-five or ninety days from Sandheads to London or Dundee, though Iredale's *Baron Aberdare* had done it in seventy, and the record was sixty-three days, but the *Bay of Panama*, headed by strong south-easterlies since she crossed the line, was 107 days out from the Hooghli when she made soundings west of Scilly under a cold and cloudy sky on the morning of 8 March 1891.

The weather thickened as she stood up Channel, and the biting east wind sent hands searching for spare jerseys and mufflers. By 2 am on Monday Capt Wright reckoned that they were nearing the Lizard, but it was never sighted as by noon sleet and snow squalls blotted out the land. The ship was now under lower topsails only, yards braced sharp up, and sailing close-hauled to the wind, the usual square-rigger method of trying to make progress against a head wind. Conditions worsened, and at 2 pm he ordered the mizzen and jigger lower topsails handed in. He could have worn ship and gone on to the port tack to leave the in-visible Cornish coast astern, but decided against it as it would have brought the ship out into the mainstream of the Channel traffic, with serious risk of collision in the bad visibility. Two hours passed, and at 4.30 pm the foresail was taken in. Shortly after 6 pm the main topsail blew out of its bolt ropes, and the *Bay of Panama* was left under bare poles. Capt Wright, convinced that he was well to leeward of the Lizard and drifting back into the open Atlantic, let her drive before the storm. In the event, it was a fatal error of judgement.

Night fell, and the wind became a howling gale; so thick was the snow that the fore lookouts could not see the tip of the bowsprit. By eight o'clock Capt Wright was begin-ning to feel uneasy, and called for all hands to hoist the staysails to try to bring the ship on to the port tack, but the *Bay of Panama*, rolling deeply in the troughs, refused to pay off before the sails were blown to rags and continued her relentless drive to leeward. Throughout Monday evening seas thundered over her decks, and the great yards and masts groaned and strained. Neither land nor beacon had been sighted for over forty hours, but at 11.30 pm two small white lights, believed to be those of a steamer, appeared briefly. The captain ordered chief officer Bullock to burn blue distress flares, but there was no reply and the lights vanished; even if the steamer had seen them, it is doubtful if she could have done anything to help the big clipper or her crew.

Half an hour later the watches were changed, and second officer Allnut joined Capt Wright on the poop, but Mr Bullock remained with them. Weather conditions were unspeakable; the icy gale seemed to cut the eyeballs, freezing water spurted down the sailors' oilers and sea jackets, and hands resembled raw meat after a few minutes' exposure. Still, square-rigger sailors stood to their duty regardless of comfort, and those of the *Bay of Panama* were no exception. Ninety feet above the deck bosun's mate Frederick Evans of Cardiff and half a dozen others swung crazily over the waves as they cleared the topsail yard. After they came down, slowly because the iron ratlines were coated with ice, Evans clawed his way up to the poop, where he stood by the helmsman. Chief officer Bullock's watch were allowed to go forward instead of standing-by at the break of the poop. Those who could got into dry clothes, and others, drenched and chilled to the marrow, huddled on their bunks. Quartermaster Charlie Higgins stretched out fully clad, and watched the guttering lamp swinging to and fro from the deckhead. An hour later he noticed the lamp take on a new and more sinister motion as the ship began to yaw and roll in short, sickening arcs. A few of his companions thought it was the tide ebbing against the gale, but the watch on deck could see what he instantly suspected; the seas that had been very high from eastwards were now shorter between the crests and more confused, as if the ship was in shallow water and tossing in the backwash from unseen cliffs.

An enormous wave curled over the taffrail, and the men

on the poop grabbed hold as it smashed across the ship, leaving the decks in chaos and the lifeboats askew. It was fortunate for Charlie Higgins and the rest of the off-duty watch that they had gone to the foc's'le. Several more great seas broke on board, and quite suddenly came a heavy rumble from deep under the bows. It was 1.30 am on Tuesday 10 March 1891, and the *Bay of Panama* had come to her untimely end.

The clipper lifted on a following sea, and came down with a crash which sent every man sprawling. In less than a minute she had pounded broadside and canted over to starboard, her decks towards the seas. (Picture, p 103.) Capt Wright shouted to second officer Allnut to fire distress rockets, and then ran down the companionway to fetch his wife from the cabin. Bosun's mate Evans battled his way forward, often waist-deep as the seas boiled over the weather rails, and though the cliffs were only 100 yards distant he at first failed to see them or the rocket which Mr Allnut fired from the poop. Evans joined the watch in the foc's'le, though it seemed little safer as the ship had begun to settle by the bows. Quartermaster Samuel McKetterick had jumped from his bunk and opened the foc's'le door, only to be flattened by a wall of water bursting around the foremast. He saw a rocket streak up from aft, but it rose no higher than the lower topsail yard before the gale beat it down.

The rocket's failure was also seen by nineteen-year-old Wallace Beresford, a Sheffield orphan and senior apprentice, who had been almost five years on board the *Bay of Panama*. He started aft, but had to leap for the shrouds as another breaker reared over the stern. Allnut disappeared, but Beresford, youthful rashness overcoming any fear of danger, swung down again with the intention of fetching his papers and savings. It was only when he discovered the way to his cabin in ruins that he realised he was alone in the gutted wreckage of the poop; not only the second officer, but Capt Wright, his wife, the cook, the steward, and one of his fellow apprentices had gone. Without further thought for his hard-earned £20, Beresford went up the jigger-mast rigging in a hurry.

The Yankee bosun was not far behind, as the carpenter and sailmaker had been carried away while sheltering with him in the lee of the midships house. Chief officer Bullock, who had been hurled over the break of the poop, crawled from under the main fife rail, dazed and shaken. He staggered aft again, calling for all who could to follow him up the jigger mast. Only half the deck watch were left to join him, and his own watch remained in the foc's'le.

It was bitterly, unendurably cold. The Arctic gale flung spray and snow to soak and half-freeze already wet clothes. Fingers hooked in frozen ratlines numbed and deadened, and eyes coated with salt and ice closed up. It became an agony even to breathe. And yet Beresford, perhaps with the resilience of youth and a little shelter from the jigger-mast top, somehow kept his senses through the long night. He watched the bosun begin to go out of his mind with the cold, and helped Forbes restrain him when he talked wildly of swimming ashore. He was quieter for a while, until he suddenly gave a wild scream and they saw him leap several feet in the air and fall, with another shriek, sixty feet to the deck below. A wave curdled across the ship and took the body overboard in the darkness.

The mizzen mast fell with a ponderous crash; soon afterwards the fore and main topgallant masts carried away, and Beresford wondered if the clipper was going to pieces. The broken spars and yards hung in a tangled mass of chains and rigging, and smashed against the side of the ship with every roll she gave. He felt her break in two and grind heavily on the rocks. The noises of the wreck became detached incidents in a nightmare, but when the dawn came it brought no kind awakening. Beside him, the boy Forbes had quietly died at some time in the night. Below, the two quartermasters who had been on deck watch, Sanders and Costain, hung one above the other like frozen puppets, and he failed to recognise chief officer Bullock's face as a swinging sheave block had killed him just before dawn. Way below, amid the ruined deck, a figure crouched by the base of the mast, and a body sprawled on the planking. Only two others, able seamen Gabrielson and Olson, still showed life and, like Beresford, looked with dull bewilderment at the scene around them in the whirling snow.

Meanwhile, Frederick Evans was also taking stock of the jigger mast, squinting through a foc's'le porthole and trying to decide whether the men in the rigging were alive or dead, when there came a lull in the blizzard and he saw figures moving about the rocks opposite the bows. He thrust his arm out and waved, and then out from the foc's'le with him came the thirteen others, drenched and exhausted, since the cross-deck bulkhead had collapsed in the early hours. Able seaman Magnus Thompson, who had left the foc's'le when the ship struck, emerged thankfully from the caboose, having spent the entire night sitting alone on the donkey winch. Then three of the apparent corpses in the rigging detached themselves and climbed slowly down. Beresford stopped on the way because it was Ingliss, one of his fellow apprentices, who sat propped at the base of the mast; he shook his arm, and then he realised that he, too, was dead. The three, haggard with exposure, stumbled along the wreckage-strewn and wave-swept decks to join their luckier shipmates. It was eight o'clock on Tuesday morning, six and a half hours since the *Bay of Panama* had driven ashore under Nare Head, two miles west by north of the Manacle rocks, and close to the little fishing village of Porthallow.

The first man to find the wreck had been William Nicholls of Penare Farm, who was wading through the snow on the headland, searching for his sheep, when he saw the great clipper on the rocks 100 feet below him. He stayed long enough to make out the figures in the jigger-mast rigging, and then floundered as fast as he could down to the village. At a few minutes to seven he was pounding on the door of coastguard William Ashley, who had come off watch at midnight but had fallen into a deep drift on the way home, and it had turned 2.30 am before he got there. Since Ashley had seen nothing of the *Bay of Panama's* distress signals, news of the wreck must have come as an unpleasant surprise, but he acted swiftly, sending word to Porthoustock before setting out for Nare Head with farmer Nicholls, several fishermen, and coast-guard Harry Giles, who would have taken over the eastern guard at midnight but had been driven to shelter.

At Porthoustock coxswain Hill knew he could not launch the *Charlotte*, as the seas were washing clean through the lifeboat house, so he saddled up his cob to go and fetch the Coverack rocket brigade. He rode into that village at 8 am, and knocked up the messenger, Joe Southey, who alerted chief officer John Gibson, a veteran coast-guard of forty-five years' service on eleven stations. He sent coastguard Allen to fetch the three horses for the rocket waggon, and as most of the brigade had been up all night, they were soon on the way, but they encoun-tered fallen trees and had to manhandle the waggon around and take the longer route instead.

Meanwhile James Cliff, hero of Monday afternoon's wrecks, and two fellow covers, Walter Matthews and Jack Hill, the coxswain's son, each carrying a small grapnel and line, had reached Porthallow to find the village deserted. At the Five Pilchards Inn they learned that every man was on Nare Head, so they tramped out through the snow to the scene of the rescue. One fisherman was already trying to heave a leaded cane line on to the clipper's foc's'le, which was only forty feet from the rocks, but the gale relentlessly blew it back. The survivors also unsuccessfully

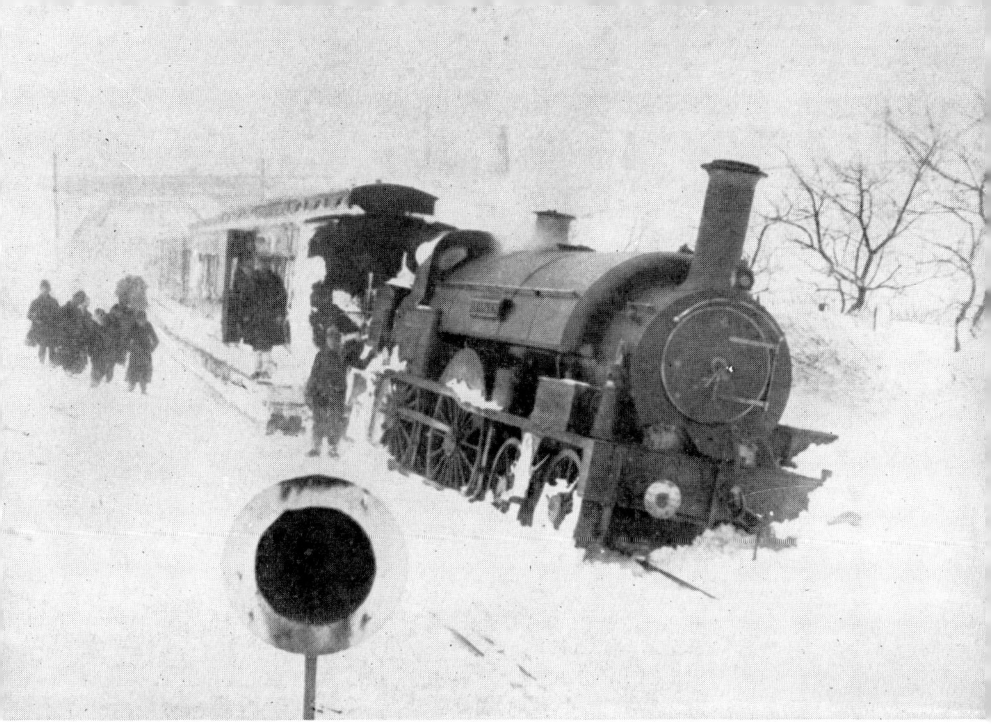

Page 85

(above) *The 'Dutchman' express with the saddle tank* Leopard *off the rails at Stray Park level crossing, near Camborne station;* (below) *A 400-year-old elm lies across the avenue leading to Mount Edgcumbe Park*

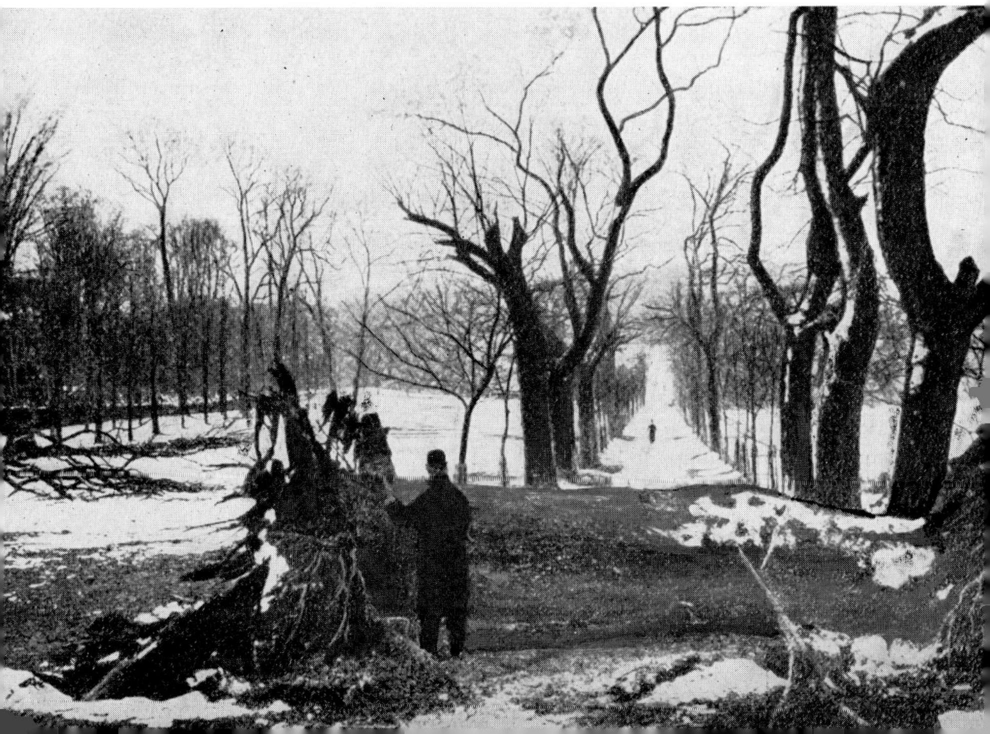

Man and horse give scale to the size of the drifts on the road between St Cleer and Liskeard

attempted to float a rope ashore tied to a spar. Fred Evans and Charlie Higgins, who were directing their efforts, then tried a freshwater tank, but this was swept away by the current. Rescue attempts thus remained unavailing until 9.15 am, when the Coverack rocket brigade came down the slopes of Nare Head.

Chief officer Gibson, who had a wide experience of rocket work, ordered the gear down to the rocks in order to get a better shot at the clipper. This was no mean feat with the deep snow and icy descent, but they accomplished it and their first rocket soared over the *Bay of Panama's* foc's'le head. As the whip and hawser were hauled off, Mr Gibson noticed the four men still in the rigging, but on asking why they did not come forward, was told they were apparently dead. Eighteen survivors were landed by breeches-buoy, all so frozen and cramped that they had to be carried up the cliff. Evans, among the last to be landed, was anxious about the apprentices aft, especially Ingliss, whom he mistakenly believed might still be alive, and asked coastguard boatman William Pond-Fisher to send somebody across. But the last man, who was ordinary seaman Wilfrid Drysdale and not the captain as Mr Gibson expected, reported that only the dead now remained on board.

Shortly afterwards, however, the coastguard officer became aware that several fishermen reckoned at least one man on the poop to be still alive. A call was made for volunteers to board the clipper, and notwithstanding the extreme danger, coastguard James Lewis was hauled off to the wreck, followed by Pond-Fisher, who steadied the line for the third volunteer, fisherman William Baker. Although the tide was ebbing, heavy seas still broke high over the decks, which were lifting from foc's'le to poop. Pond-Fisher handed his lifeline to Lewis and went down into the cabin, but found it gutted, with all the bunks smashed down. He and Lewis then climbed up to look over the break of the poop. A ghastly sight met their eyes. The heights of the mast were blotted out by a squall, but in the lower rigging they saw the two quartermasters, swinging stiffly with the roll of the ship, and another man lay face down and rigid on the deck. At the foot of the mast Ingliss was down on one knee, his arm hooked around the rail, and his eyes wide open and staring sightlessly into the driving snow. All were obviously beyond human aid, but just to make sure Pond-Fisher shouted and waved at them several times, and getting no response he and the other two returned ashore.

After hearing their report, chief officer Gibson ordered the rocket line cut and the gear taken back to the waggon, ready for any other call which might easily come during the day. Yet there were many who still genuinely believed that the apprentice crouched under the jigger mast was alive. Francis Tripp saw him turn on his side and hold up an arm; Joseph James was convinced that he bent forward on to his hands and knees, and said so to coastguard Giles, but received a blunt reply. Henry Nicholls thought the apprentice waved his hands and then slumped back against the mast, but admitted that as it was still blowing so hard, the movement could have been caused by the rolling of the clipper. Something of an argument ensued between Gibson and one William Roskruge, who evidently insisted that the coastguards should fire another line on board, and when told it was impossible as there was no one to secure it on the ship, asked for a volunteer to swim out. James Cliff stepped forward, but Gibson was reluctant to let him attempt what he regarded as such a hazardous and pointless risk of his own life. He did order his men to stand by the lines, although he warned Cliff that he tried to board the *Bay of Panama* on his own responsibility, and the rescue bid went no further, though the young fisherman's bravery was indisputable. An atmosphere of some dissension prevailed as the men dispersed.

Up at Penare Farm the *Bay of Panama's* survivors were thawing out around blazing fires, and they recovered sufficiently to tramp the two miles up to St Keverne village, and at 3.30 pm they boarded a horse bus, provided to take them to Falmouth where it was thought that they would be better lodged. A few hours later, and only five miles away, the bus lurched into a deep drift at Gweek.

Meanwhile there had already begun an epic journey which over the years has become a legend of the blizzard of '91. At 1 pm Joseph Hendy James, son of the St Keverne butcher, started out on his pony to take news of the wreck to Helston. The snow still whirled about him as he crossed the bleak expanse of Goonhilly Down, but he reached the town and a young clerk, Alfred Oates, met him leading the pony down Meneage Street. Oates, who worked in the office of Capt Phil Richards at Gweek, had himself been out in the blizzard on Monday evening. As he started out for home he had been surprised to find the tide flooding through the village and whitecaps breaking over Gweek bridge (five miles from the sea up the Helford river). The first two of his four-mile tramp home had the shelter of high Cornish hedges, but Oates was soon struggling along in the hurricane. Trees plastered with snow took on new and frightening shapes, and all the time was the howl of the storm; if it had not been blowing against his back the boy would probably never have reached Helston.

Josephy Hendy James found only bitter disappointment in Helston, as the town was cut off and every telegraph line down. Nobody would have blamed him for seeking shelter or going home, but he resolutely turned his pony up the highroad to Falmouth. The drifts got deeper, and he had to leave his exhausted mount at a wayside cottage. Still he kept going, walking along the hedgetops or wading waist-deep through the snow. As darkness fell the daughter of a stonemason named Combellick saw him crawl up to the front door of their cottage. He was so exhausted that they at first thought he was dying, and they put him to bed, but at dawn young James resumed his trudge to Falmouth. Although the morning was clear he was soon on hands and knees again, but at 8 am he reached the offices of Messrs. Broad, the shipping agents, and delivered the first news of the wreck below Nare Head.

Four hours later, a few minutes before noon, a strange and pathetic procession of eighteen shivering scarecrows, two on one horse, two in a pony trap, and the rest straggling behind, many on bootless feet which were blue with the cold, wound its way along Falmouth High Street towards the Royal Cornwall Sailors' Home. The survivors of the *Bay of Panama* had arrived.

COMPLETE LIST OF THE CREW OF THE 'BAY OF PANAMA'

Officers and others on deck at the time she struck

Captain David Wright	Sailmaker	
Mrs Wright	Carpenter	no record of names
Chief officer Bullock	Steward	
Second officer Allnut	Cook	

The watch on deck

Bosun	* Gabrielson	able seamen
* Evans—bosun's mate	* Olson	

* Beresford	Rogers	
Forbes	Smith	ordinary seamen
Ingliss	Brown	
Allport	Weston	

Sanders	quartermasters
Costain	

The watch below

* Higgins	quartermasters
* McKetterick	

* Thompson	* Blackler	
* Collins	* Williams	
* Hawkins	* Carpenter	able seamen
* Mulbrae	* Mactier	
* Fitzgerald	* Jansen	
	* Logan	
	* Drysdale—ordinary seaman	

(Thompson, Collins, Hawkins, Mulbrae, Fitzgerald — able seamen)

* survivors

6

Tuesday: dawn to dusk

All the earth was flat with snow, all the air was thick with snow; more than this no man could see, for all the world was snowing.
  —R. D. Blackmore, *Lorna Doone*

Tuesday dawned and the blizzard was still sweeping the western counties, and the bitter cold was unrelieved by the ENE gale which had blown at near hurricane force for sixteen hours. From Land's End to the Mendip Hills townspeople and villagers alike discovered that their homes were surrounded by huge drifts, which obliterated familiar roads and lanes, and even large streams and millponds. Up on the high moors, where hard winters were customary, the farmers faced conditions which even their great-grandfathers could not have recalled.

Exmoor lay cut off from the rest of the world by five to fifteen feet of snow, though one lone traveller had reached his moorland home just as the blizzard gained strength. Farmer Ridd of The Barton, near Simonsbath, had driven into Porlock on Monday morning but was uneasy about the weather and made sure to leave early. He reached Wellshead Farm, near Exford, and there left his pony trap and tame lamb; as he started for home he told the Wellshead people 'If there's anybody behind me they'll never get through.'

And there was someone behind him, twenty-year-old Amos Cann of Greenland Farm, near Simonsbath, homeward bound after selling a horse at Porlock. He ignored pleas to stay the night, and disappeared in the driving snow up Porlock Hill towards Exmoor. Three weeks later his scarf was found on the common, and his body in a ditch only half a mile from his home. He had in all probability slipped while climbing over a hedge under Alderman's Barrow and died of exposure.

So blinding was the snow on Exmoor that night, that Shepherd Balmond, who had worked at Wellshead since a boy, almost lost his life just a short way from the farm. He was tending his ewes in a small field when a gust blew out his horn lantern 'and though he knew every inch of the field, it was a long time before he found his way back'.

Twenty miles away, the snow-filled dark hours had turned Dartmoor into an Arctic waste. Farmsteads were marooned and sheep and ponies buried. Princetown village and the great prison cowered under the blast of the gale, which had unroofed a dozen cattle sheds, torn off part of the church roof, and heaped up immense drifts in every direction. At the prison officers' school several of the moorland children slept peacefully before roaring fires, unable to return to their snowbound homes. Monday night's branch train still lay buried in Eggworthy cutting, but the rest of the Princetown people were better off. Although the village was fairly well stocked, animals from the prison farm were slaughtered for meat.

On the opposite side of the moor forty-seven volunteers had begun shovelling their way from Chagford to Moretonhampstead, the terminus of the GWR branch line from Newton Abbot. Fifty others started out towards them, but it was a fortnight before they met halfway between the two villages. Meanwhile the railway was blocked, but just before dawn three snow-covered figures had arrived at Moretonhampstead station, and yet another small but epic battle against the blizzard became known. Some days previously J. and W. Dicker, millwrights of Chagford, had held a sale behind the ancient Three Crowns Hotel to dispose of a large steam engine and boiler. The weather was warm enough for the men in attendance to carry their jackets over their arms, a good indication of the suddenness of the blizzard. A Kingsteignton clayworks bought the engine and G. H. Reed of the Rushford works, Chagford, steam haulier and thresher, was hired to dismantle the machinery and transport it by traction engine and heavy waggon.

All was ready by 11.30 on Monday morning, and the convoy, preceded by a man carrying a red flag, set off for Kingsteignton at the regulation 4 mph. By the time they reached Bovey Tracey, at 1.30 pm, the snow was falling and freezing as it fell. The steersman could barely keep his heavy load on the crown of the road, but they struggled on and reached Kingsteignton shortly before dark. By then the snow was deep enough to preclude any idea of returning to Chagford with the traction engine, so the fire was raked out, the boiler emptied to prevent it freezing, and the three men set off for home on foot. The roads and lanes were almost unrecognisable in the darkness and snow, but as they crossed the branch line from Newton Abbot they saw that the rails, being on an embankment, were relatively clear, and they walked along the line to Moretonhampstead station and thence to Chagford.

Just across the river Teign from where the Rushford men left their traction engine, the little village of Combe-by-Teignhead was covered in deep snow; drifts piling up against doors made them impossible to open and great icicles hung from the thatched roofs. The village blacksmith and his young apprentice had to dig their way up to a well some way from his home, as it was the only supply for several cottages. Afterwards they cut a path across the main road, to rescue the family's grandmother, and the smith's then small daughter still remembers looking across the fields and river to Bishopsteignton and Kingsteignton and seeing the 'wonderful white carpet of snow'.

This second morning of the blizzard was to remain in the memories of other south Devon children. The thirteen-year-old son of the village shopmistress of Lee Mill Bridge awoke to find his home

> ... completely covered and Mother called me to see what the noise was about outside, the room was dark, I lit a candle and went downstairs, it was 9 o'clock and we used to open from 7 am till 10 pm and after. The men of the village were just clearing the snow away from our shop door, the first words they said were 'Ban't ee gwain open shop today?' They soon cleared the bread, pork, candles and oil, all went.

The shop stocked everything—boots and shoes, medicines, clothing, oil, pitch, tar, paints and brushes, maize, barley meal for pigs—but did not bake bread, and later in the morning the boy walked two miles to Ivybridge and managed to 'scramble home with six 8lb loaves'. By then the roads were so bad that he was not allowed to go out again, and the village men themselves went to fetch more.

Another child on Dartmoor at the time remembers

> ... my father being cut out of a deep snowdrift on his horse, into which they had sunk on the way back from Holne to Luesdon. He was there for two or three hours until a farmer found him and he was dug out ... I also remember that the butcher's cart was in our courtyard for nearly a week unable to get back to Ashburton. The snow was level with the hedges and the moor was a wonderful sight.

For most West Country children the blizzard was a great excitement.

> I was a small boy . . . living at Broadhempston about four miles from Ashburton. My mother and I walked about a mile on the road as far as Waydown Cross, towards Ashburton, when it started to snow so we turned back . . . I recollect seeing my uncle shovelling the snow away from our bedroom window, it was as high as that. I know we couldn't go to school for a fortnight. I suppose we small boys had a lot of fun.

The ten children of the village carpenter at Kingston, above Bigbury Bay, tumbled downstairs to watch their father trying to open the door:

> . . . It was quite exciting for we children . . . the snow was six to eight feet deep, we could look in upstairs windows, in fact my wife (then eight years old) took bread over the snow to the bedroom window of an old couple.

This little girl had a particularly eventful day, as she also saw people carry in a donkey which had been snowed in and was unable to walk, and while playing with other children she fell through the snow where some sheep were buried, which were then found by the searchers.

Down on the coast the sea-fronts of the south Devon resorts showed the effects of the wild night. At Paignton, the landing-stage of the promenade pier was washed away, the sea wall in front of Redcliff Tower was undermined, and the Volunteer Artillery ammunition shed was wrecked. At Dawlish, probably the worst hit of all,

> . . . the fishermen and others of this attractive watering-place sustained great losses by the destruction of fishing and pleasure boats. At the Coastguard Station the boat-house was partially unroofed, and large blocks of granite

were hurled a great distance...the Ladies' Bathing Pavilion, which stood on the beach in front of the Marine Parade, was carried away by the sea, and almost entirely destroyed.[1]

Brixham harbour was in chaos, 200 feet of the breakwater and its light-pedestal had gone during the night, and the shore was littered with broken fishing gear and debris from gutted boatyards. Most of the fishing fleet had dragged or parted their moorings. The 22-ton cutter *Energy*, DH 265, drove in the stern of the Torbay hooker *Florence;* the mumble bee *Laura Mildred*, DH 291, was badly damaged; the 47-ton cutter *Bluebell*, launched by Samuel Dewdney only three years before, capsized and crushed her entire side on the rocks, and the *Prince of Orange* almost drifted out to sea. In the inner harbour every craft broke loose. The *Unique* and the *Vigo* telescoped their bows on the jetty wall, and the *Alice* finished up with her bowsprit almost thrust into the noble eye of the Prince of Orange statue. Although over forty craft were damaged, only one was wrecked, the 48-ton smack *Quiver*, owned by Joseph Furneaux, which drifted from the outer harbour on to Fishcombe Point. The 14-year-old craft broke up, and even as her wreckage came ashore the trawler *Pioneer*, manned by a crew of five, trailed her single bower anchor close to the point. At 10.30 am the lifeboat *Brian Bates* put off, and as the gale lulled for half an hour escorted the trawler back home.

The Brixham fishermen themselves sprang to the rescue around four o'clock that afternoon, when the 185-ton brig *Emile*, Vigot master, eighteen hours out from her home port of Cherbourg with general cargo for Guadeloupe, drove into Hogg's Cove, near Berry Head. Led by chief officer Drayton of the coastguard, they landed eight Frenchmen, who were taken to the nearby home of the Misses Hogg, leaving the *Emile*, launched by E. Lecerf of

Cherbourg in 1875, fast breaking up. To get the news to the brig's owners, a sixteen-year-old baker's boy volunteered to ride a pony to Dartmouth but when he reached Hill Head above Brixham he realised he would never get through on the pony. So he put it into a nearby farm and fought his way through, 'mainly walking on the tops of hedges'.

When the boy reached Dartmouth he found the town cut off by very deep snow, and the telegraph system in such confusion that the message to the London agents had to be sent via New York. The Kingsbridge coach had got in on Monday night only with great difficulty.

> I shall never forget the drive home to Dartmouth [said driver Saunders in later years]. There were only four passengers, two ladies and two men, and the coach was one of the smaller ones with four horses...the winds sweep over the Ley road with such terrific force that the coaches ran great risk of being overturned...ballast was usually taken up at Torcross and put out again at Strete Hill where the opposite coach picked it up on the return journey. That night I thought I could do without it, but soon found out my mistake...it was a heavy struggle across the sands, and I suggested to the two gentlemen that they should sit on the windward side, and that the ladies should sit on their knees. In this way we kept the coach upright and reached Strete Gate in safety. I forgot to tell them when the danger was over, so when I saw them again they said, 'You told us to sit like this for your own pleasure, and now we have stayed for ours!'[2]

After the excitements of the night in Plymouth Sound, dawn brought the wreck of the 30-ton ketch-barge *Kate*, which had just discharged at the St Keverne Stone Co's wharf at Mountbatten when she parted from three anchors in a heavy squall. Away she went before the gale, missed

Drake's Island by dint of the crew hoisting the foresail, but struck under the Italian Gardens at Mount Edgcumbe. They threw a kedge anchor to leeward and jumped ashore, then waded through the snow to 'Lady Emma's Cottage' where they were soon enjoying a hearty breakfast sent down from the big house by Viscount Valletort.

The Plymouth fishery was at a standstill, and from Tuesday morning the fishermen's children were given free meals at the Bethel Mission, while many of the younger crews spent the day snowballing each other and passers-by around Southside. Anxiety was caused by the non-appearance of the trawler *Electric*, which had sailed on Monday morning and was last seen by the *Excelsior* twelve miles SE of the Eddystone Light, but around noon she limped into Sutton harbour, having spent the night in the lee of Rame Head.

The blizzard had brought the same night of misery and hardship to east Cornwall, where drifts blocked light from downstairs windows of many cottages. Baker Ware from Looe had had to abandon his cartload of bread at Longcross, near Tratford Farm, where farmer Julian waded through the snow to rescue his sheep. The youth who was 'living in the house' was too frightened to accompany him, but he safely brought in ewes and their newly-born lambs and put them alongside a pile of corn in the barn.

The memories of another local boy illustrate how alike were the experiences of every farming family.

A brewery firm from Liskeard sent their horses and wagon with supplies to Lanreath Punch Bowl Inn. They struggled along as far as our farm at the top road and got bogged down, so they unhitched their horses and got on their backs and returned with them to Liskeard, leaving the loaded brewery wagon in the middle of the road about two miles short of their intended destination ... (it) remained there for weeks. My family were engaged for days digging out of the snow new-born lambs and their mothers. My father's family and his two brothers' families were fortunate in that the day before the blizzard they had taken to their homes flour from the grist from their own wheat, which had been taken to the mill some little time before.

Monday had been market day at Liskeard, and many homeward-bound farmers were caught out by the blizzard. Farmer Hancock and his son Harry were returning to Menheniot with a cow and calf and 'had to carry the calf the last mile as the snow had become so deep that it could not walk.' On arriving home they had to stand in front of the fire to thaw out before they could remove their clothes as they were covered in icicles.

Deep drifts on St Cleer Down blocked the reservoir leat which supplied Liskeard, and it took twelve hours' hard shovelling to remove the danger of a water famine. Between St Cleer and St Neot some drifts were sixteen feet high, and roadmen had to cut a track for horses and carts through snow which in places 'was an arch above their heads'. Not all the roads were as bad as this, but most were filled with snow, and near St Austell a doctor's coachman riding horseback with his master was injured when his horse went over an invisible hedge.

Fowey and Par were inaccessible by land or sea; at Mevagissey, the new £20,000 breakwater had taken a tremendous battering, and none of the trawlers or hookers dared face the great seas bursting across the harbour mouth. One pilchard driver caught far out to sea ran for home, but struck the Yawl rock off Gorran Haven and drove on to Great Perhaver beach. Skipper Joseph Solomon and his crew jumped ashore, but the driver and her haul of 12,000 pilchards were engulfed by the waves.

A dozen miles distant the Falmouth boatmen and sailors were still contemplating the devastated harbour when, at

7 am, the lifeboat maroons crashed out for the second time in twelve hours. The schooner *Agnes and Helen* of Beaumaris, cement-laden from Faversham to Newport, drove beyond Maenporth on to the ragged ledges between Bream Bay and 'Gatamala' Cove, where thirty years before the Baltic timberman *Guatamala* had also fallen to an easterly gale. Capt Jones, who had been at the wheel since driven from the Downs with a score of other coasters fifteen hours before, mate Pritchard and able seaman William Roberts jumped overboard and waded ashore as a breaker recoiled. Coastguards brought the exhausted Welshmen through the drifts to the Royal Cornwall Sailors' Home on Custom House Quay, where they were the first of a dozen crews to be given shelter during the blizzard.

Falmouth, like every other town and village, was cut off; shops, schools and offices remained closed, and the busy shipping business was paralysed. One or two Penzance luggers came in, but the only large ship to arrive was the 576-ton Norwegian barque *Abbe*, Olson master, salt-laden from St Ubes, leaking and minus her mizzen mast and rigging. A few hardy souls did try conclusions with the 15ft drifts. The Rev Deshon, hoping to conduct a funeral at Constantine, had to be dug out of the snow just beyond Penryn, and a few miles further along the highroad a party bound for the same village to attend an auction were marooned in a farmhouse with their cab horse. Farmer Christopher Midlen of Tresahor, near Constantine, was lost in a field he knew well, wandering bemused by the blizzard until rescued by William Thomas, who worked at Treglidgwith, by which time he had icicles 'hanging from his whiskers to his knees'.

A man who tried to reach Falmouth was Mr Hugo of the Redruth Posting Co, who started out at 9 am in a two-horse wagonette, but after covering only two miles ran into huge drifts on the hill above the mining village of Lanner. No train had left Falmouth since the one which connected with the ill-starred 'Dutchman' express; station-master Hocking kept a light engine ready with steam up, though there was little hope of her getting through the deep cuttings behind the town. At the other end of the branch line Truro was a ghost city; shops opened but no customers appeared through the swirling snow, the cathedral clock refused to strike because of the cold, and the only indication of life were the 'enlivening strains of a German band'.

The hurricane was also roaring across Mount's Bay, and during the morning some of a fleet of sail that lay anchored in Mullion Roads ran for Penzance. The Truro schooner *Morwenna* skimmed the capsized dock gates and drove on to the harbour sands, and the Harwich schooner *Wesley Park* arrived badly damaged with her captain lost overboard. The tug *Flying Serpent* brought in the Bridgwater schooner *Saltram*, and with her the news that she had almost collided with a crippled Garibaldi schooner off Longships, but was herself too disabled, with her captain, Felix Agrippa Rudge, dying from injuries, to give aid. Without doubt she had seen the last of the *Prima Donna*, the only Garibaldi-rigged schooner known to have been off the West Cornish coast that morning.

The Penzance lifeboat *Dora* nearly capsized on going out to the Newcastle schooner *James Nicholson*, slate-laden from Caernarvon to Bergen, but four lifeboatmen managed to get aboard and run her into Newlyn. This was not a particularly safe place, as the strong run of seas sent the luggers crashing and jolting together. The *Nyanza* and the *Dauntless* were tossed ashore, and soon after the *James Nicholson* arrived, the lugger *Catherine* recklessly ran for Penzance. A gust broke her mainmast and she drifted down into the rocky corner under the Tolcarne Inn, but a hundred fishermen laid hold of ropes and hauled her bodily up the beach.

On the windswept hills above Penzance and in the fishing

villages around Land's End, miners, farmers and fishermen awoke to find themselves in a state of siege. Madron, St Buryan, Lamorna and Sennen, where a coastguard look-out almost froze to death, were beyond reach. Near St Just, the drab grey mining village overlooking Cape Cornwall and the Atlantic, 'Thomas's bus', a four-wheeled vehicle resembling a western stagecoach, lay axle-deep in the snow. It had left Penzance on Monday evening, but failed to climb the steep hill at Crows-an-Wra. Driver Willie Hall and two passengers turned the horses loose, in the hope they would find their own way home, and asked for shelter at a nearby cottage. They were refused, and climbed back on board the bus, huddling miserably together in the bitter cold.

At daylight the haggard, snow-caked figure of William Penrose, farmer and Wesleyan preacher of Bojewyan, a mining hamlet near Pendeen, appeared outside. He had, according to his own account,

> ...left home to catch the nine o'clock coach to Penzance...about noon at Truro it began to snow, and continued to do so during the afternoon and night. The wind was terrific, the snow was fine and blinding. I shall never forget the sight of the snow blowing while in the train, and the cold we endured, but what was that to what I endured afterwards? Having arrived at Penzance I...found that the bus had left early on account of the weather...I went back to Mr Woolcock's restaurant and partook of a good meal, and...felt half-hearted about leaving. I left...about 7 pm. Mr Woolcock offered to lend me a walking stick...and...I remember asking him if he would provide me with a bed should I come back. 'Yes' was the answer but having started I had no thought of turning back, but many times regretted having made the attempt. When I came to Alverton, I took across Castlehornic fields. Every now and

Page 103

The tragic wreck of the Liverpool jute clipper Bay of Panama *belcw Nare Head*

Page 104

(above) *The main street of Beacon village, near Camborne, on Wednesday;* (below) *the German steamer* Carl Hirschberg *high and dry at Portloe where she stranded on Monday night*

then I was on my hands and knees in snow ... I got across to the main road with difficulty. When on the road the hedges were my guide, and I could not miss my way. The snow was six feet deep on the road in places. I reached Tremethick Cross and thought of stopping, but no, I was homeward bound.

Several times he hesitated, wondering whether to call on friends; at Newbridge he 'looked towards the Public House, and had I been accustomed to visit such places I expect I should have pulled up'. He stopped again at Trig-the-wheel Hill, but then pressed on, branching off across Drycarne.

I made a big mistake by going over Drycarne. I had no hedges for my guide and I was getting in the drifts. The cramp was taking hold of me and I was gasping for breath ... and I resolved to turn back. I had something then to face the wind and fine snow, and had to walk backwards. I thought I had gone far enough to be on the St Just main road, when I beheld wheel-tracks leading into a field. I thought I had gone a little out of my course, but it turned out to be the spot I thought. I felt then that it was no good for me to wander, having made a halt I could not think of moving. I stuck the walking-stick kindly lent to me into the hedge for a mark. The wind was coming through the gap so fiercely that the snow was being blown away. I began to jump and keep jumping for a while. Then I began to sing Hymns, what Hymns I cannot tell, but this I say, I believe I never sang more sweetly. I counted the minutes for how long I cannot tell, then I got against the hedge and took off my overcoat and put it over my head. I felt my breath a little warm at first ... but soon it had little effect. When against the hedge I kept constantly beating one foot, then the other in the pit of snow which I had made for my feet and legs. Although I was there in that state I thought I was better off than many poor sailors ... I was there I should think about eight or nine hours in one place. I thought I would not be there for all the money in the world. I was asked by an old man how I felt, when death seemed to be staring me in the face, about the past, present and future. I told him I was battling with the present and hoping for the future. I thought I might be benumbed at any moment. I was told once about the Guardian Angels being over me. I should think they were on that occasion; I almost thought at times I could see them.

Sometimes in the middle of the night I was prompted to shout, so that if there were any persons at a reasonable distance they would hear me. I almost fancied I heard voices, and I think now I did, as Mr Archelaus Thomas's bus was not more than a couple of stone throws away from where I was, with five people in it. It must have been near six in the morning when I tested my legs, to find out whether I could walk. I was close to the main road. I then walked backwards to the house the St Just side of Tregerest Chapel. It was very difficult for me to get near the door or the window, there being such a bank of snow there . . . the lady of the house answered (my call). I told her I had been up there hours and wished to be taken in. I was told 'It is coming light now and you can go home' . . . Then I started for St Just. What I took to be a miller's wagon . . . turned out to be Mr Thomas's bus . . . I went to the door, I to pull and they to push from inside; it was tight with the frost . . . I got inside; and they felt the cold coming in after the door had been opened. They said 'Throw down your oiler to keep the wind out', to which I replied 'That is no oiler, that is an overcoat'. It was a tweed one frozen stiff. I said 'Had I been in here it would have been grand'. They told me that they had been complaining. They would not admit having heard me calling, but admitted having heard me singing . . . in . . . a very short time I began to burn, and cannot describe my feelings . . . So I went on. Having passed Jericho (farm) gate, the road was full of snow. I knew I had enough, even although it was light, and if I got into the drifts I should be done. I went down across the field to Jericho and tapped the latch of the door with my stick, and said 'Open the door, I want to come in, I have been out all night.' I would not be turned away then. They asked me who I was from the bedroom window, I said 'Penrose'. Mrs Thomas told me afterwards she said 'He is not the Penrose I know, he is looking too old'.

Mr Penrose is quick to excuse the woman who turned him away, as her own husband was stranded away from home, and unstinting in his gratitude to Mr and Mrs Thomas, who gave him peppermint water to drink, took off his boots, Mr Thomas having 'spent years in America and understood about being frost-bitten', put him to bed and got breakfast for him. In his own words, 'I went to Jericho and fell among friends'.

Few people voluntarily spent the night out, but one who did was James Murphy, chief officer of coastguards and coxswain of St Ives lifeboat, who kept watch from the Island lookout. Down in the harbour the recently extended pierhead sheltered both coasters and luggers, though heavy seas inundated Westcott's Quay. Jenkin's carpenter's shop was gutted, and the artists' club upstairs had to be evacuated; the Warren was flooded out, and the fishermen's families spent a cold and uncomfortable night. The gale also demolished more of the old wooden breakwater, which was eagerly scooped up for firewood by the poorer people.

Despite the blizzard, no rockets or flares glittered in the bay, though a large steamer and a barque came dangerously close to the land, but at 8 am a schooner was seen ashore on Hayle bar, and as all telegraph lines were down, no one could discover the fate of her crew. Chief officer Murphy was unable to launch the lifeboat because of heavy seas, so he ordered the rocket waggon to Hayle. At noon the men returned, plastered with driven snow from head to foot, having been baulked by a massive drift at Carbis Bay. Even if they had negotiated this one, another, 200 yards long and 9 feet deep, blocked the road a mile onwards at Lelant It had already bagged a four-horse wagonette, its driver and four young girls who had rashly tried to travel from Goldsithney into St Ives. They were rescued by a Lelant mine captain, who also had their horses dug out and taken to the Praed Arms.

Early in the afternoon, as the tide ebbed, the schooner's crew splashed stiffly through the shallows. She was the 83-ton dandy-rigged *Perseverance* of Preston, thirty hours out from Swansea to Salcombe with coal, which had run for Hayle in the small hours but missed stays and drove under Black Cliff. The weary sailors were led across the dunes, upriver to the harbour and the Steam Packet Hotel, haven for all shipwrecked crews on the bar.

Only a few hours later came word of another wreck, when farmer John Nicholls reined up his cob outside the Hayle custom house. Shortly after midnight the 129-ton Fleetwood schooner *Alice Crookhall*, Ratcliffe master, Cardiff for Jersey with coal, had crashed over the rocks and shingle in Mutton Cove at Godrevy Head. Her crew, sighting land for the first time in ten hours, scrambled ashore along the jibboom and scaled the 100ft cliffs. Capt Ratcliffe recognised the flash of Godrevy light, but there was no shelter except for a hut into which they all squeezed. When daylight came they reached Godrevy Farm, carrying an elderly sailor. The *Alice Crookhall*, launched at Irvine in 1874, and whose plight was hidden from the vigilant coxswain Murphy by Godrevy, was left rolling herself to pieces in Mutton Cove.

No ship had gone on to the dreaded Doom bar, but the

bows of the schooner *Louisa* had demolished the galley and bulwarks of the Bideford schooner *Ballinbreich Castle* as they pitched at their moorings off Padstow harbour. The ground seas piled up by the offshore gale were enormous; throughout the night two young artillerymen and their families cowered in the battery house on Gun Point, expecting every minute to be swept away. At dawn their garden had gone, and every loose object had been blown over the cliff. In the harbour a boat weighing over a ton had been flung high on to the jetty, and traffic out of the town was halted by deep snow. The blizzard had claimed one life during the night. Rebecca Chapman, returning home to Crugmeer after collecting her parish pay and staying late to shop in Padstow, was so bewildered by the storm that she wandered through a field gate and collapsed, and her body was found under the snow several days later.

Port Isaac, Boscastle and Tintagel likewise huddled under the blizzard, and the Bude coach could not cross the moors to Holsworthy. Over the Devon border the hamlets of Hartland parish were lost to the world. At Bideford, Ilfracombe and Barnstaple, the townspeople had little to be thankful for as Tuesday's dawn revealed the thickly falling snow. Monday evening's train, the 6.38 pm from Exeter, lay embedded in Barrow cutting, on the steep incline above Morthoe station. Her fourteen passengers had struggled back and been given shelter at stationmaster Grover's house and the Fortescue Hotel.

These same great drifts had nearly claimed a farmer's lad from Fullabrook, who rode seven miles to fetch medicine from Dr Manning of Combe Martin. On the return journey he was 'blown from his horse and dragged by one of the stirrups a considerable distance', but kicked himself free and returned to the doctor's house; his horse was later found 'partially entombed by the snow' but unharmed, and he was able to ride home.

In Combe Martin Bay the 195-ton brigantine *Ethel* of

Salcombe, London to Newport with general cargo, had driven under Hangman Point in the early hours. Capt Hockin and his five crew rowed ashore, guided by the backwash from the invisible cliffs, but the *Ethel*, launched by Date of Kingsbridge in 1876, was a complete wreck. Three miles away the Padstow schooner *Pride of the Bay* lost her mainmast under Hillsborough, but was rescued by a tug.

Out in the Atlantic, as on land, the blizzard was still raging unabated. The elderly 183-ton Aberystwyth brig *Crusader*, Williams master, Caernarvon to Hamburg with slate, was abandoned ten miles off Trevose Head with seven feet of water in her hold. For nineteen hours the Welshmen drifted to a sea anchor, and Tom Owen, an old sailor, died of exposure just before they were rescued by skipper Albert Gempton of the Brixham trawler *Gratitude*, thirty-five miles south-west of the Bishop Rock.

The blizzard continued to exact its toll in the English Channel. The 67-ton schooner *Biltine* of West Hartlepool, with a cargo of beans from Maldon to Poole, drove from her anchors in Weymouth Roads on to Preston beach. Another elderly coaster, the 32-ton smack *Lord John Russell*, was wrecked in Studland Bay. Further to the east the 13-ton Newhaven lugger *James and John* was tossed into the surf west of Littlehampton, and also lost on the Sussex coast, near Felpham, was the Exeter ketch *Western Belle*, whose four crew were rescued by the coastguard whaleboat, commanded by chief officer William Fitzgerald. Yet another vessel lost off Dungeness was the 59-ton Goole schooner *George William*, inward bound to Rye with paraffin and nitrate of soda, which sank in heavy seas, though Capt Ely and his crew were rescued.

There was great anxiety for the Kentish fishing fleets after Monday evening's wrecks at Hastings, but all the Folkestone luggers returned except one, the 15-ton *Welcome Home*, which was blown far to leeward and struck near Seaford. Her master, William Burt, and his four crew jumped ashore safely, facing huge snowdrifts on the downs above, where a coastguard on nearby Beachy Head had frozen to death during the night.

Tuesday's last shipwreck was the 34-ton Padstow smack *Porth*, culm-laden from Swansea to Penzance, which had left Mumbles Roads late on Monday afternoon in company with the *Prima Donna* but lost sight of her when the blizzard caught them off Trevose. The *Porth*, severely damaged, was blown past Land's End, and at five o'clock on this stormy evening after recognising the flash of the Bishop Rock light, her master, Joseph Billing, hoisted a scrap of mainsail and made for St Mary's. But the little smack was slowly settling, and he was trying to beach her on Annet when she struck an offshore rock.

Mate Charlie Box, a powerful swimmer who in 1885 had been the first man to swim the mile from Newquay pier to Porth Island, jumped on to the reef. The *Porth* then washed free, and Billing and his son launched the boat and rowed to Annet; the craft was sucked back, and the boy only saved his life by seizing his father's leg. They were rescued by St Agnes lifeboat, but there was no trace of Charlie Box, only twenty-nine and just a year married. Although registered at Padstow, the *Porth* was a Newquay coaster, owned by Richard Bennett of Porth, where she was launched in 1877.

So ended Tuesday, a wretched day for the West Country, but not before an incident at Tiverton bore witness to its severity. The first part of a newspaper train which had been snowed up all day near the Whiteball tunnel, halted at a home signal for a few minutes, and in that short time froze solidly to the rails. By midnight the blizzard was moderating, but this was little comfort to marooned villagers, or to passengers trapped in the stranded trains, for none could tell what the morning might bring.

7

Wednesday: a lull

Wednesday's dawn brought a welcome change. Gone
were the gale and driving snow, and a light westerly breeze
ruffled the drifts which sparkled in the sunshine. This
picture of placid, Alpine-like calm was marred by the
numerous funnels and carriage roofs which showed in the
blocked cuttings, by the abandoned vehicles, and the acres
of devastated woodland. The big country estates and
noble parks of Cornwall and Devon had been severely hit,
and stewards, servants and keepers gazed sombrely at the
ranks of fallen trees. One landowner at least wept un-
ashamedly at the sight.

In Mount Edgcumbe park, overlooking Plymouth Sound,
two thousand trees were down, and enormous gaps in the
woods were easily visible from the Hoe. (Picture, p 85.)
The east-facing beechwood had taken the brunt of the
gale, especially around 'Lady Emma's Cottage', where,

throughout Monday night, a young gardener and his family had cowered, listening to the roar of falling trees and expecting every minute to be crushed. Fortunately for them a great beech immediately to windward remained upright, though less exposed trees had brushed the cottage eaves in their fall. The beautiful English and Italian Gardens looked as if they had been trampled by a giant's feet, and the celebrated orangery narrowly escaped destruction from a collapsing elm.

Although in a more sheltered position up the Tamar valley, the woodlands at Cotehele were so badly damaged that the house could be seen from Calstock for the first time in living memory. Elms, sycamores and ashes had been uprooted or broken, many in the glade which fronts the house towards the river. The lovely walk from Cotehele Quay lay in ruins, and in the surrounding woods over 100,000 cubic feet of timber had fallen. Some of this was later used by James Goss, shipbuilder of Calstock, to build the ketch *C.F.H.*, one of the latter-day British coasters. Only Cotehele's oaks had held to their roots; a coppice of them surrounding the ancient chapel of Sir Richard Edgcumbe, in spite of its perch on a rocky height above the Tamar, survived the hurricane unharmed, though other stalwart trees had succumbed around it.

Cotehele House had also suffered greatly. The inner courtyard resembled a crowded graveyard as scores of slates off the roof had embedded themselves end-on in the snow. William Coulthard, the earl's head steward, has left a graphic description of Monday night.

> ... The noise of the storm resembled the frantic laughter of millions of liberated maniacs, broken at frequent intervals by what sounded like the deafening and rapid volleys of heavy artillery, and, as these died away, louder and louder rose the appalling screams of the storm, with slight intervals of lull and perfect calm,

only to return with tenfold violence, which made the whole house tremble and vibrate.[1]

At 7 pm two heavy skylights were blown off the kitchen roof, and soon after that a chimney came down. This was only the beginning of the steward's trials; several of the east-facing windows were later blown in or shattered by flying branches, and even when the broken panes were blocked with old books, crates and canvas, snow rushed in, until the corridors had 'to be cleared like the pavement in the street'.

A mile downriver the grounds of the 200-year-old Pentillie Castle were in a worse state. Rare ornamental shrubs had been blown clean away or buried deeply under the drifts; fallen trees blocked every path and walk, and months were to pass before the debris was cleared up.

The blizzard had also swept up the valley of the Tavy, and the Rev T. W. Wintle of the riverside village of Bere Ferrers was appalled at the desolation revealed by Wednesday's glorious sunshine. The gale, which had sent a chimney crashing into his bedroom on Monday night, had also blown down or broken off nineteen of his firs and oaks, ruined the rectory garden, and scythed flat a nearby cherry orchard of a hundred trees.

Only a mile upstream on the opposite bank of the Tavy, fifty times this number of trees were down at Maristowe, the home of Sir Massey Lopes. Destroyed was the famous avenue of limes from the croquet lawn to the tennis courts, and fifty large beeches lay prostrate across the drive. Near steward Merson's house, where he and his family had spent Monday night like the gardener at Mount Edgcumbe, in constant fear of being crushed by falling trees, stood two old and decayed sycamores due to be felled. Came the blizzard, and every tree for acres around, including a monarch elm and a stout 6oft fir, was levelled, but the two old sycamores remained upright.

Across the river from Maristowe a firwood three hundred strong had been reduced to a score of battered trees, and two miles farther up the Tavy valley Sir Francis Drake's ancient home of Buckland Abbey stood surrounded by 15ft snowdrifts and ravaged timber. The extensive Rookery between the north and south lodges had been flattened except for a few elms, all damaged by the gale or by others falling against them. Half the beeches in the avenue on the abbey's north side were down; centuries'-old trees, including a venerable sycamore which had shaded many a pleasant tea-party, followed the beeches, and the fine old cedars and some of the famous tulip trees were shattered or uprooted.

One of the extraordinary escapes of the blizzard was that of a farmer and his wife who were caught by the storm while visiting Place Barton Farm, beside the Rookery. They decided to leave early, and as the south drive was already blocked, drove off towards the north lodge. Just as they reached the limit of the Rookery, 'down came the last tree over them without warning, and, marvellous to relate, the horse, conveyance, and occupants were imprisoned between the large branches . . . without the slightest damage whatever being done'.[2] They were released with some difficulty, and accommodated at the lodge until Wednesday, the pony being stabled in the kitchen. Soon the trees scraping the back bedroom roof of the farm, afterwards the whole of the Rookery came down, one of where a child lay asleep.

The lodge keepers and stewards of Buckland Abbey, like the Rev Wintle of Bere Ferrers, were among many people to notice the erratic nature of the hurricane. In places it had carved a circular swathe a quarter of a mile wide through the woods, and in others a narrow twisting path. Some gusts appeared to have descended vertically and uprooted, or twisted the tops off, elms and beeches, yet left others alongside untouched. Further confirmation of these freak cyclonic conditions came on Wednesday morning, when the Norwegian galliot *Falken*, Johannes Maland master, was towed into the Cattewater by the Plymouth tug *Belle*. Bound from Shields to Camphia in Portugal, she had left Dungeness roads on Monday morning, and at eight that night, twenty miles south-west of Start Point, Captain Maland, running before the ESE gale, suddenly realised that the snow was driving directly towards him from westwards.

The 'intervals of lull and perfect calm' noted by steward Coulthard at Cotehele, and by Capt Maland on the *Falken*, were also reported by Capt Andrew Haggard in Devonport. In a letter to the *Western Morning News*, he wrote:

The cyclonic nature of the blizzard that has been annoying us all so much, and causing such a frightful amount of damage during the last two days, may be judged by the following observations taken by several officers in the South Raglan Barracks on the evening of the 9th instant. From these observations it would seem as if for a time the South Raglan Barracks were in the exact centre of the storm, being left for varying periods in a complete calm in consequence. Here are the notes we made: At 8.12 pm the storm was raging so furiously that the solid old Raglan was shaken to its foundations, the fire was roaring up the chimney as if in a blast furnace, and the noise made by the blizzard generally was such that it was difficult to hear one's neighbour speak. But at 8.13 suddenly came a complete lull. The elements ceased to wage war, the fire assumed its normal demeanour, and an officer who went out to see what had happened came in and reported that it was so calm he was able to light matches outside. For thirteen minutes did this calm last. At 8.26 with a roar like thunder, the wind returned, and once more we were dreading that the armies of the chimney pots would fall upon us in their fury. Only for twenty minutes, though, did the hurricane scream and yell, and as before make itself generally obnoxious. At 8.46 there was another absolute cessation of wind until 8.53, when it 'blizzed' worse than before. And shortly afterward everyone started forth to put out fires, when all the amateur meteorologists discovered to their grief that whatever the cyclone might do in the way of lulling occasionally down at the Raglan, on the top of Stoke Hill it blizzed all night with perfect impartiality.

Hardwick Lodge

The bright sunshine revealed more desolated woodland around Saltram House, Lord Morley's country seat, where 400 trees were down. Gamekeeper W. J. Lockyer, who had feared for the roof of his home, Hardwick Lodge, was out with under-keeper Charlie Palmer when they found and rescued a man lost in the snow. At Walreddon Manor, near Tavistock, the picture was the same, and the Rev H. D. Nicholson, who had recently returned from visiting relatives in Newfoundland, had to make use of a pair of snowshoes he had brought home with him in order to get together a party of men to dig the drive out, which was completely blocked with snow. (Picture, p 137.)

So many trees had fallen around Widey Court, near Crownhill, that after the blizzard a sawyer's pit was made at the side of the main drive for the purpose of cutting up and planking trees. Mr Charles Fox, who lived there, had had a narrow escape on the Monday night, when, unable to use his carriage because of blocked roads, he walked home from Ford Park. When at last he reached the lodge in a state of complete exhaustion, it was only to learn that the lodgekeeper had been found dead in a snowdrift just outside.

Lord Revelstoke's mansion of Membland faced Bigbury Bay and the blizzard, and when his wife, her niece and staff ventured forth, they found the house front thickly coated with frozen snow, ivy leaves on the north wall encased in bells of ice, and the creeper hanging in glittering festoons. Outside the main door stood a 14ft drift, and on Tuesday the lodgekeeper had taken two hours to cover the threequarter-mile driveway to the house. The drive itself was cratered and torn up by the roots of falling elms, and on the estate another two thousand trees were down, including valuable ilex and oak.

Elsewhere in the two counties many people left their homes for the first time since Monday, but few got very far through the drifts. There was no post or newspapers, coal, flour and meat remained undelivered, and with the country people marooned the weekly markets were abandoned or had little on their stalls. Stocks of food were dwindling, and prices in the towns were rising; at Bideford the people had to pay 2s 6d per lb for butter.

Most of the Cornish turnpikes were impassable, but Bazeley's of Penzance succeeded in getting a waggon hauled by four pairs of Shires and with eight men shovelling through to Hayle. Beyond the town drifts blocked the road, and another heavy waggon which Hosken, Trevithick & Polkinghorne Ltd sent hopefully off to Camborne foundered on the steep hill above Roseworthy. One of their drivers, James Rule, who lived in this little hamlet, had to 'get out of the bedroom window and walk on the snow to Loggans Mill' (all for eighteen shillings a week, on which to support seventeen children).

Camborne was at a standstill, offices, shops and schools stayed closed, and much damage had been done to the shrubberies round the villas in Basset and Pendarves Roads. The Truro-bound horse bus and a barrel organ were among the trail of abandoned traps and carts on the highroad to Redruth, and all the surrounding villages were inaccessible. Baripper Lane was filled from hedge to hedge; near Kehelland stood a 30ft drift; at Pengegon the cottagers had to melt snow as the pumps were frozen, and down at Penponds, where all hedges had vanished, undertakers men had to manhandle a coffin over the snow to a house. The author's great-grandmother, Eliza Jane Date, was snowed up with her three daughters in her cottage on Copper Hill. So deep was the drift that her husband, returning from shift at South Condurrow Mine, where he was 'engine man', had to shout 'Are you there, Eliza?' down the chimney.

Other Troon mines, Wheal Grenville, Newton, and West Francis, where the adventurers' meeting had to be postponed, were badly short of coal for the boiler fires of their pumping engines, and for three days there was a serious risk of flooding. The fire stamps were also slowed down, and tin-streaming and all surface work was halted by frozen snow which choked the buddles, leats and waterwheels. A lad named Wallace, who worked at West Francis, failed to arrive home at Carnkie after Monday's shift; a search was made, and his body was found in a drift only yards from his front door.

Throughout Tuesday's blizzard and Wednesday's

sunshine, Capt Rich and the South Condurrow miners dug their way through the drifts until a passable track ran between walls of snow ten feet high up Mount Pleasant to Beacon village, and thence over Greenland Hill to the mines at Troon. Up went laden coal wagons from Camborne railway yard, hauled by roughshod ponies, the heels of their hind shoes turned down to give a better grip on the ice. On the other side of Camborne, miners from North Roskear had eventually to dig their way across Tehidy Downs to fetch coal which usually came by wagon from Portreath. The only mine with adequate coal was Carn Brea, but the miners refused to deliver it, and the manager, purser and clerks had to wheel it in barrows down to Cook's Kitchen and East Pool. There was also trouble at Penandrea Mine, above Redruth, where men who refused to go down because of the cold were fined. The following shift struck for the fines to be remitted, but the manager was adamant; eventually, after the money was sent to the miners' hospital, they agreed to work.

Over in South Devon and wading through the drifts towards Totnes was Capt W. H. Angel, who had been one of the passengers on Foale's bus which had left the King's Arms Hotel, Kingsbridge, at 5 pm on Monday for Kingsbridge Road railway station. The eight travellers, including a couple on the way to be married, were very crowded, but soon glad of the warmth. At Loddiswell a lady alighted, and an official of the Exeter telegraph department who had been surveying the lines came aboard.

Until then the storm had not been too bad, but a quarter of a mile beyond the village the bus came to a halt, and 'a shapeless mass of snow, with a human being in the middle' appeared. It was the driver, and as he opened the door a rush of freezing wind covered the passengers with rime. Bluntly he told them he was going no further. 'I can't see my horses; it is snowing in sheets, and there is a drift in front across the road four feet high.'[3] The offer of five shillings, soon increased to ten, and the company of someone on the box beside him, persuaded him to continue, but a few hundred yards later the bus stopped again. The driver reappeared in a blast of wind and snow; 'It's of no use, gentlemen; we are stuck.'

Rescue was improbable, and they decided to abandon the bus. The driver unharnessed the horses and struggled off with them towards Blackwell Park Farm, though it was dawn before he reached safety, and the passengers set out for the California Inn. On arrival the snow was already so deep that they had to creep in beneath the lintel of the back door. A dozen other fugitives from the storm were already ensconced, but landlord Jackson and his wife rose to the occasion. The bride-to-be, who had been dragged through several drifts, was almost hysterical, though she calmed down after a glass of brandy. As her trousseau was with the rest of the luggage on top of the marooned bus, Mrs Jackson lent her some clothes. But 'the bride', Capt Angel records, 'was what you would call a fine woman, tall and stout. Our landlady was somewhat short and decidedly slim ... but delicacy forbids me saying more, and the readers must imagine the rest.'[4]

A spare room was set up as a dining hall, and the weary people demolished a ham and egg supper; then, as sleep was impossible, they sat around the fire telling stories and riddles, and occasionally singing. At daybreak the inn was snowed up to the front eaves, but at 8 am, despite Mr Jackson's protestations, Capt Angel and four others decided to make for Kingsbridge Road station. Within yards of the back door they sank waist-deep, and had to skirt a 15ft drift before they could cross the fields to the highroad. The gale blew straight into their faces, and after a quarter of a mile one man gave up and returned to the inn. Capt Angel and Messrs Sparrow, Soper and Smith, pressed on, walking on hedgetops, and here and there sliding down banks of snow or floundering chest-deep, chanting 'We Traced His Little Footprints in the Snow', until they reached the station at noon. While drying out in the coffee room they discovered how little they had advanced their case in the absence of any trains.

After a most uncomfortable night, but considerably cheered by the sunshine and a hearty breakfast, the party separated, the captain heading for Totnes, hoping for a train home, and the others for Plymouth. The morning was quiet and calm as he tramped across the snow, and he met few people; the occasional farmer searching for his sheep, and later some of the telegraph corps repairing the wires. When at last he entered Totnes late in the afternoon, wet and exhausted, to his disgust he was 'welcomed by the gamins in the street as a fit subject for snowballing'. He found the Dartmouth river steamers idle, and not until 7 pm did he get passage on a launch belonging to HMS *Britannia*.

Also stamping through the drifts on this sunny morning were fifty men from the village of Malborough, near Salcombe, searching for Thomas Arnold, a farmer's boy missing since Tuesday afternoon, when he had been sent from Furzedown to another farm in quest of some lost sheep. After darkness fell his anxious parents had raised the alarm, but no search could begin until dawn. Fortunately the boy had had the sense to crawl into a gorse bush and put his oilskin jacket over his head, and there a Bolt Head coastguard found him sleeping at 10 am.

A few miles up the coast Lt Bridger of Salcombe coastguard, J. C. Nye, deputy receiver of wrecks, and the editor and a reporter from the *Salcombe Gazette*, were heading for Prawle Point to investigate the wrecks. Above Portlemouth village, where 3ft icicles hung from the thatch, they took to the hedgetops, but one or other of the party frequently tumbled into the snow. At Portlemouth Farm a Prawle man who had come to fetch bread agreed to guide them, and after a gruelling journey they reached the Union

Inn, where they seated themselves before a roaring fire to interrogate the survivors of the *Marana*.

Breakdown trains had been rolling out since early morning, and of all those abroad the hundreds of railway gangers had the hardest time. Just before 8 am the Truro and Lostwithiel men freed the special which had lain all night in a cutting near St Blazey Gate. Shortly afterwards a lone express engine arrived, the pilot of a parcels train from Millbay which had been delayed by upset goods wagons at Devonport and a derailed broccoli train at Doublebois, where frozen signals had to be worked by hand. As the way was clear she returned to her train, which reached Truro four hours late.

The Truro gangs were also active on the Falmouth branch. Two tank engines and a brake van were skilfully manoeuvred by drivers Uren and Newcombe through the blocks around Perranwell, and arrived at Falmouth at noon. The telegraph was still useless, but at 5.25 pm a train went up to Truro to connect with a mail, though this only got as far as Liskeard.

Meanwhile other engineers and gangers were trying to rescue Monday night's perishable goods train from the snow outside Redruth. The breakdown train, hauled by two heavy goods locos, Nos 1232 and 2155, encountered the engine at Scorrier behind a huge drift. They backed into the snow to reach her, but it offered less resistance than expected, and in the resultant collision William Richards, a young brakesman of Burngullow, was flung from the step of No 2155 on to a signal wire post and badly injured. The conditions around Scorrier were particularly bad, and on the previous night three young gangers seeking shelter found a bal maiden frozen dead in the snow. In spite of the accident the Truro gang cleared the buried engine with an hour's energetic spadework, and reached the 'perishable' at Treleigh. One van contained twenty-five pigs, which had been fed by porters from Redruth for the last two days. The wagons were re-railed before a large crowd of eager spectators, and early in the evening the combined trains steamed into Redruth.

A similar bid to open up the Par to Newquay branch line was less successful, for although a breakdown train passed through St Columb Road, heavy drifting stopped her at Cosworth. Behind her came Monday night's train, twenty-eight hours late, but even so her mails could not be delivered until carriers' carts got through to the station from St Columb town. All the surrounding moors and lanes were lost under snow so deep that a lad in a pony trap was lucky to be rescued by another traveller.

The Bodmin branch line had also lain silent since Monday evening, after a Wadebridge-bound tank engine was abandoned near the beginning of her journey, but success met the efforts of Capt William Sowden and the Calstock miners, who cleared the East Cornwall mineral line to Kellybray. Calstock, though well sheltered by the Tamar valley, had caught its share of the hurricane. Trees were down by the score, making the tracks leading through the woods to Buralston station nearly impassable, and Mr James of the Passage Inn had most of his famous rose trees destroyed. Surprisingly none of the tall mine stacks had fallen, though the engine-house roof of Drakewalls mine was partly blown away, and a large shed in James Goss's shipyard collapsed. One violent gust upset the 250-ton iron schooner *Naiad* in Danscombe Bottom under Kelly Rock, but her masts fouled the river bank and stopped her from capsizing; she survived to be lost off Looe in another March gale forty years later.

On the Devon railways, gangers sweated in the sunshine as they burrowed into mountains of glistening snow. Superintendent Compton stopped off at Torridge House during the morning to visit the two drivers, of whom Murray had temporarily lost the use of his legs and was badly frostbitten in one foot. His and Coleman's engines had been salvaged, but whole lengths of the line were still buried, and not far distant Anne Farley, a miner's wife, had died of exposure on Monday night while returning to Plympton after visiting her father at Hemerdon.

The branch from Exeter to Teignmouth was opened up at 5 am when an engine plough and carriage found Tuesday night's local train fast in a drift beside the boathouse of Powderham Castle, her few passengers having spent the dark hours beside a roaring fire in a gangers' hut. Another engine and plough pushed into Tiverton early in the afternoon, allowing a Paddington express to reach Exeter. Yet another breakdown train sliced through snow ten feet deep to Moretonhampstead, and returned to Newton Abbot to fetch mails and passengers, but those destined for Chagford had to continue on horseback.

The Somerset & Dorset Railway had also been largely immobilised since Monday, and though a few trains ran on the Bridgwater and Wells branch lines, an early morning workmen's train on the Evercreech-Burnham branch became marooned despite the aid of three engines. A train which did reach Burnham stuck at Highbridge on the return journey, and when a double-header sent out to help her also failed to get through, all operations were called off. Some of the worst blocks were in the Mendip Hills around Masbury summit, where the s & DR, after a long climb from Radstock and Binegar, dropped down to Shepton Mallet. Monday night's up goods from Evercreech had gone into a drift near the Bath Road viaduct; a down goods failed on the sharp, icy incline from Shepton to Cannard's Grave summit, and was rescued by a breakdown gang and by navvies engaged on doubling the main line. Several engines and scores of men were busy throughout Wednesday in trying to restore some semblance of normal traffic between Bath and Bournemouth; even dynamite was used on some of the deeper drifts, but as on the GWR and LSWR, it was a slow, uphill battle, soon to be lost again.

Many of the stranded passengers seized the opportunity to try to get home. Four businessmen walked to Launceston from Okehampton. Seven other travellers, four of them women, armed themselves with spades and walked from Morthoe station across the fields to Ilfracombe, arriving just after lunch. Several of the 'Zulu's' people, tired of their hungry sojourn at Brent, where boredom was only relieved by helping the marines and soldiers fill the engine boilers, set out for Plymouth along the railway line. Their pace was slow, especially around the cuttings, where they took to the field hedges, but at Ivybridge they were given hot cocoa and tea by Mr Compton's men and on various relief engines ultimately reached their destination.

Up on Dartmoor the passengers of Monday night's branch train from Princetown had at long last escaped from their exile in Eggworthy cutting. After the guard and engine crew left on Tuesday morning they had huddled together miserably until 3 pm, when three gangers arrived from Dousland with cocoa, bread and butter and cake, and a bottle of 'well-watered brandy', welcome but sparse fare for people who had not eaten for over twenty hours. Before they left, the gangers brought the lamp from the guard's van; one man asked if he might accompany them back to Dousland, but on being told that it would take several hours, gave up the idea. The passengers gloomily faced their second night of the blizzard, but after midnight the weather moderated and at sunrise they saw farmer Hilson of Horsford Farm digging sheep out of a drift. Although his home was only 250 yards away, he had seen nothing of the train in the blinding storm. Messrs Hancock, Viggers, Palk and Worth later walked to Dousland, and the train was left roof deep, the compartments filled 'above the hat racks' by snow which had sifted through the windows and ventilators.

Some miles away, at Horrabridge, Mr Weekes and his

fellow travellers had spent an equally comfortless night in the little station waiting room:

I studied the texts on the wall 'A man shall be a hiding place from the wind'. Another text made me feel that perhaps I should never reach my earthly home—'Watch, for the Son of Man cometh in an hour when ye think not', and another about His coming suddenly.

It was so difficult to know how to spend the time. I read two advertisements on the wall over and over, about Insuring in an Accidental Assurance. Out of the window we saw that 'Newberry's tea was the best' and wished we could try it! I read a newspaper through, even scanning the advertisements, looking at the date last I found it was January!

The earlier part of the night seemed windier than ever. A newspaper stuffed in under a door blew out again with a pop. I had to put a handkerchief over my head and keep on my hat, so great was the draught. The wind, however, fell and by daybreak stillness reigned and the stars shone out. The morning was perfect—a cloudless sky, air lovely. A telegram came from Yelverton, bade the gangers be ready, the engines were getting up steam and would cut their way through to us.

9 o'clock—no engines. We looked right away almost to Yelverton station and saw the steam of the engines evidently working away at the drifts.

This was a relief train commanded by Inspector Northcott which had left Millbay at 8 am, and among whose complement was Dr William Square, bound for Yelverton to see a patient. It reached Horrabridge after many stops, one when Northcott himself was swept off the running board by a frozen drift and fell under a wagon, at great risk of losing his legs. But by the time it arrived Mr Weekes had decided to seek his own salvation, because

... the Wesleyan minister (Mr Nicholson) who was one

of our party went off to Tavistock and I thought I would make my way to Mr Fred Butt's. So, walking along the railway cutting and climbing up the signal-post ladder, I reached the field adjoining his garden and then over the railings I made for 'The Brake'. I saw peeping thro' the snow the top of a garden seat which I passed and soon found myself before the dining-room window where Mrs F.B. was looking out. She was astonished to see me and only wished she had known and her servant man could have helped me to their home for shelter. I had the luxury of a wash, the first since Monday! I felt very shaky when I first sat down but Mrs Butt was as kind as kind could be and bacon, eggs and coffee rapidly disappeared and I was quite refreshed.

I consulted their servant man (a retired Princetown warder) and he thought that to attempt to walk home *alone* a dangerous task. So I left 'The Brake' with the intention of getting down to the engines to see what was to be done but reaching Mutton Corner I felt so revived by the glorious Dartmoor air and my good breakfast that I determined to try and walk home.

I found the snow frozen and crisp, each footstep making a crackly sound. The sun was shining brightly overhead making the snow almost dazzling. I went at a good pace hoping to overtake someone. I stood still once and listened—there seemed an unusual silence, not a sound could I hear. On I went again and getting warm carried my overcoat and pocketed my gloves. Of course I came across some drifts but could generally walk on the heaps of earth running along the side of the road. The average depth of snow on the road to Roborough was not more than six inches.

A mile or so past the Rock I met Mr Bellamy coming out to see the leat. In answer to my question he said it was 'a bit roughish by Roborough'. Also met three on horseback and two or three walking. Two men were clearing a drift and two came across the moor from Bickleigh direction and stopped to speak to the labourers as I passed. The view of the long stretch of snow-covered hills was grand. All around I could see tokens of His power and felt within tokens of His love.

When I descended from the moor I thought 'Now will come the struggle' so I ate a couple of sandwiches which Mrs B. gave me. She also gave me some Brandy but I knew that my safety depended on my clear-headedness and was afraid to touch it lest it should go up into my head. I remembered Captain Webb and abstained. Mrs Butt made me put on a pair of thick stockings over my boots and trousers to keep the snow out. They answered admirably and seemed to keep quite dry until I came to Roboro'. Entering the road from the moor is a thick wood on the right. Numbers of great trees lay rooted up. Nearing Roboro' I had a choice of mounting a snowbank or walking in a stream—I chose the latter.

Roborough looked like a place closed. The houses were covered with snow, no windows showing, only the dent where one knew the window should be. Trees scattered about in all directions. The snow had now become much more wet which made the walking very fatiguing. Some way after Roborough I met a postman coming out. He told me that the road farther on was blocked and that I must go over the hedge into some fields and I should find the road again. He showed me some red footprints in the snow. He said 'These are my footmarks, I came across a field of red earth. Follow these marks and you will be all right.' I kept closely to the instructions and only once had to retrace my steps and then only a few yards. Up went the red marks right over a high snowdrift, up and up until I looked down on the hedgetops. Step by step I followed putting my feet in the marks made by the postman, consoling myself with the thought 'where he had walked I can walk'. I came to the ploughed field. There was scarcely any snow here on the ground. All the snow had blown over into the road which looked like a huge bed covered with a snowy white counterpane. The ploughed field took away my strength terribly—the earth clung thickly round my boots until I could scarcely lift my feet. Over a hedge and across another field with a drift at the end— I had to descend some way in order to reach the top of a gatepost to get into the road again. Here someone had cleared the snow from the front of the gate. I walked over some good high drifts but always found some feet-marks to walk in, rarely sinking deeper than my knees. I met Charles Radford on horseback. He was working his way to Yelverton where he was lodging—I was able to direct him through the fields. Later on I met Arthur Popham whose horse had sprained his legs, so sending the horse home he walked. I then came across a poor tired-out postboy, bound for Plymouth. This was my first companion since leaving 'The Brake' at Horrabridge. He had tramped miles and miles over the country and seemed 'done up'. I gave him the rest of my sandwiches of which he made short work. At Crown-hill we had again to leave the road and take to the fields.

Knackersknowle was a sight—it seemed as if the enemy was surrounding the village and barricades of snow had been thrown up for protection. A gentleman here offered me a lift which I gladly accepted and we drove under a regular succession of arches formed by the trees falling across the road and being caught by the opposite hedge. My ride came to an end where the Devonport road turns off, and stepping down I found it wet and cold to the feet. I caught up to my friend the postboy who had walked on, the carriage did not start from Knackersknowle for five minutes. Going up Winstone Hill I felt terribly tired but kept going on at a steady pace, walking on mechanically. Mannamead put a little life into me and I made a spurt to Mutley. Coming in I met Miss Polkinghorne and the two Miss Wilsons, and was obliged to apologise for my state. The feet of my stockings I had worn through and I was splashed from head to foot! I've no doubt I looked a perfect picture as I had not brushed my hair or shaved since Monday morning and it was now Wednesday afternoon. I went past Mutley station in case any of my Anxious ones might be there. I passed down to the Gordon Terrace so that I might be seen from my house some distance approaching. Wearily I dragged my tired limbs up the last bit of hill, the snow here was about a foot or more deep all soft and wet. Some boys were playing snowballs and I was about to shout 'Wait a moment until I pass' but had not energy enough to speak so passed along and received not a single shot. I heard a shout from my house followed by yells of joy. Patterings of feet, kicks, scamperings and all were out the next moment at the door waiting to welcome the lost traveller.

While Mr Weekes was making his escape from Horrabridge, a large body of gangers had reached the last victim of Monday night's blizzard, the abandoned 6.38 slow train from Exeter (Queen Street). The men in the brake van had spent the night shivering around an improvised brazier, a bucket filled with coal from the boiler fires, and at Tuesday dawn guard Moore and fireman Oates had tried unsuccessfully to get food from Sourton Inn. No help was forthcoming until noon, when the mayor and half a dozen stalwarts came from Okehampton with food and brandy. By this time 'the train was entirely buried on one side, the engine having forced the snow . . . up to a height of fully twenty feet.' The women and children were assisted to Youlditch Farm, and the rest were 'marched back to Okehampton at a swinging regimental pace' by one of the passengers, George Pearse, at that time a major in the 4th VBDR, 'singing at the tops of their voices in marching time.'

The Exeter gangs also cleared Meldon Junction, and an LSWR pilot engine forged through 7ft drifts around Halwill to go down the branch line to Holsworthy. Her crew were the first outsiders the townspeople had seen since Monday, as they were besieged by enormous drifts which had swallowed hundreds of sheep and cattle. In Holsworthy itself there was a drift twenty feet deep and 300 yards long below the railway arches in Chapel Street. All the water mills in the district were frozen into their ponds and leats, and William Stidwell of Shop Court, Milton Damerell, walked eight miles with half a bag of wheat on his back across fields, rivers and hedgetops to Torrington and the only steam-driven mill for miles around. But by late Wednesday afternoon the sun had retired and the slight thaw ceased, and dark clouds were once more piling up in the east.

8

Thursday, Friday: more snow

The weather worsened throughout the night, and Thursday 12 March dawned piercingly cold, with storm clouds flying before the rising north-east wind. Despite the renewed freeze and threat of further snow, a heavily laden special from Exeter steamed into Devonport Junction at 7.30 am. On board were the first mails to reach Plymouth for over sixty hours, including many GWR bags which had been salvaged from their stranded trains and sent back for shipment on the LSWR. That the mail had got through was due to the untiring efforts of the relief gangs still shovelling between Lydford and Meldon. Stationmaster Hocking of Tavistock had taken advantage of the dozen engines immured there to send all available men up the line, and though the snow often reared six feet above the pilot's smokebox, by 1 pm on Wednesday they were under Brent Tor. By dusk, when the weather broke, much of the line above Lydford was open. Reinforcements came when a train which had taken stranded passengers down to Devonport returned with fifty company men, well armed with food and shovels.

Although only the up LSWR line was in operation, eager officials at Devonport organised a rough timetable to clear the enormous backlog of parcels and passengers. An up express left for Waterloo an hour after the Exeter mail arrived; on board were scores of commercial travellers, and the West India and Pacific mails, seventy-six bags and fifty-two parcels, landed at Plymouth from the Royal Mail Co's liner *Atrato*. This train did eventually get through to her destination, but another which was being marshalled amid the slush and ice was to be less fortunate.

Meanwhile, divisional superintendent Compton and his men had left Millbay at 7.15 am on the heels of another Launceston relief train, but lost precious time when their engine was derailed on Hemerdon bank. At Cornwood they were gratified to learn that digging towards them were two hundred gangers and a plough, which had reached Totnes the previous night from Swindon. Other navvies from the new Brent to Kingsbridge branch had been labouring through the drifts with them since 5 am, and they had cleared around the 'Zulu' express, much to the delight of the remaining passengers who were by that time heartily tired of the station and its elderly master.

Both parties moved steadily on, and at 11 am Mr Compton, having walked ahead to meet Swindon officials at Ivybridge, telegraphed Paddington on the newly restored wires that he hoped the GWR line between Plymouth and Newton Abbot would be open to traffic by late afternoon. But even as the message went out gangers, drivers and brakesmen paused in their work and stared skywards as large snowflakes began whirling down. The blizzard had returned.

Bowlers and caps were pulled down, mufflers re-wound and collars turned up; during the next few hours the cuttings still reverberated to shouts, engine whistles and the clash of couplings as the breakdown trains resolutely inched forward, until at 2 pm Compton's men and the Swindon gang met around Monday night's mail train in Langham cutting. Then, as one of its coaches was re-railed and hauled back down the line, disaster came out of the driving snow. A relief train from Millbay screeched around the bend. Driver Waye, who had been misinformed that the breakdown gangs were at Ivybridge, was travelling fast to cut through the drifts, and too late he sighted the gangers. His engine knocked the stationary coach bodily from the rails, lost its funnel and smokebox door, and careered violently to a halt against the embedded train.

Many men had been at work under or on the mail train, and the cry of 'Look out! Train coming!' came too late. They were 'scattered in all directions, several of them being buried in the snow'. Foreman Storey of the Plymouth locomotive depot and ganger Willcocks were dragged out badly injured, and William Stantiford, aged twenty-eight and newly married, was found dead under the front wheels of the mail engine, which had been propelled several feet forward across the line. Compton rallied his shaken men, but discovered that the line behind them had been blocked again, and reluctantly gave the order to stack shovels. Wearily the men climbed aboard the trains, sharing what food they possessed with the Swindon men, who had hardly eaten or rested since leaving Totnes.

The return of the blizzard had also seriously hampered the Launceston relief train, which had recovered Mr Weekes's train and towed it back to Horrabridge before tackling 15 and 20ft drifts around Grenofon tunnel. She reached Tavistock and ultimately Launceston around 4 pm, where her arrival was noted by Miss Rose Arundell of nearby Lifton, in her observant account of what the great blizzard had brought to that district.

Monday March 9th 1891 [she begins] At about 12.30 a slight wind and a little rain. Mama and I went to Launceston (with others) by the 1.7 train, and home by the 2.19; by the time we reached home the wind had risen and snow was falling and it was bitterly cold. Wind continued rising and snow falling all afternoon, nevertheless Thomas Bradshaw kept his engagement of dining with us here, going home at 10 o'clock. By that time there were thick bands of snow all over the windows and a thick coating on the ground. The hurricane raged all night and all next day (Tuesday) and we could see nothing from the windows but a blizzard, driving every way, and immense deep drifts everywhere. The roof was loaded with snow, Wm. Penwarden went assisted by George to clear off as much as possible. We found there was no mail arrived and trains were stopped and buried *somewhere* in the snow. The mail cart started last night driven by Weevil and accompanied by Dyer, and tandem horses for Bridestowe. The storm was terrific all this day and no one seemed to be about in it. We heard that the day before Maurice Doidge had been to Lew Down to see a patient and that it was so blinding that he and his man had to take it in turns to drive, for a very few minutes each, and then protect their eyes.

On Wednesday was a most lovely day, the storm having completely subsided in the middle of the night. I put on Walpole's gaiters and my thick boots and ulster and started out in the morning. I went to see different people and enquire for them and saw everywhere being dug out. After seeing them, I went down to Underwood, and found the drifts that way very big and the river at Blackypool one sheet of thick snow which had been driven up. Back from Underwood and round by Leat and to Colman's Cross where again were enormous drifts all in beautiful and fantastic shapes—some like a stormy sea with huge waves curling over, and just arrested in falling and with frothy crests. Others hanging over and above the hedge like great lions' and tigers' heads. On further up Tavistock Road (Whitely Hills) there was a

Page 137

(above) *Snow encrusting the walls of a room at Walreddon Manor, near Tavistock, the window having been left slightly open during Monday night;* (below) *a road near Brent shows the condition of most West Country lanes, even when cleared, for many days after the blizzard*

Page 138

A view of Hughtown, St Mary's, showing, although the snow has begun to melt, that the Scilly Isles had their share of the blizzard

block and I met Mr Northey from Lake who told me he had walked down over the drifts which went over the hedges and that people were employed cutting a place for horses and people but no wheels can possibly get that way. Between Southern Bridge and the station in the road it seemed like a great platform, just about up to one's shoulder, but the wind had kindly left a tiny passage close to the hedge, just room enough to walk through on the same side as the Mays' cottage. Up the New Road the wind had taken the snow round and round which gave the appearance of wedding cakes in some and the others being scooped out looked like so many hip baths. In the afternoon Mama came with me round Leat and up the New Road to admire the wonderful sights of billows and caves and rolls and twists of every sort.

It is interesting to compare Miss Arundell's observations with part of R. D. Blackmore's description in *Lorna Doone* of the great winter of 1684: 'The great drift was rolling and curling beneath the violent blast, tufting and combing with rustling swirls, and carved (as in patterns of cornice) where the grooving chisel of the wind swept round.'

Nothing heard of mails or trains [continues Miss Arundell's account] except a rumour of one being broken down at Horrabridge. Mrs Cross was buried during yesterday afternoon in the storm and today little girl Mounsden. The snow had to be cut away for a path and for the grave.

Splendid snowfights today. The snow thawing and pouring in through various places.

Thursday. Still no return of Weevill and Dyer, and no telegraphic communication further than Tavistock and Launceston, and no trains till the afternoon and then only engines with breakdown relief men to try and clear the line and also one tried to get to Plymouth but had to return, but this day they had some news of the mail: to the effect that the bags had reached Bridestowe on the men's backs and that the cart was broken down at a place called Stonefarm. In the morning just before 12 o'clock the postwoman at Launceston sent a 'special' mail being a light dogcart from Millmans with tandem horses to try and reach Bridestowe, having earlier in the day sent cartloads of men with shovels etc to dig out a way. Not much use as they could only reach Stonefarm and no outside letters had reached there. Bakers' carts

'Bakers' carts were going about tandem'

were going about tandem, and the Spry Mills waggons went to Launceston with three and four horses, the roads towards there being better—and during this day I went towards Stone and found the hill completely blocked but walked up over the drift over the hedge. People could walk or ride that way by careful management. Also I visited the station and while I was there the stationmaster telegraphed as far as he could (Horra-bridge) to enquire for the train which they had heard had left Yelverton, but it had again left the rails.

The fresh snowfalls had also brought further tribulations to the GWR in Cornwall, but a variety of parcel and passenger trains reached Truro from Millbay, and an up London mail had passed through at an early hour. On board was an agent of the Eastern Telegraph Co of Porthcurno, who carried nearly 3,000 messages, two days' backlog caused by heavy drifting which cut the cable station off from Penzance. Truro was still a beleaguered city; the busy mid-Lent fair brought only a few stallholders on to the streets, and for the third successive day the mail carrier failed to reach Perranporth. The telegraph line to Falmouth was still dead but the branch line was kept open by railwaymen determined not to see it close even though the renewed blizzard was sweeping the countryside.

Equally determined efforts had begun on the Gwinear to Helston branch, where sixty gangers boarded a brake van and two open wagons, which were backed into the drifts by a powerful tank engine. Led by the tall and stalwart figure of their chief ganger, William Clymo, who, as a young miner in the 1860s, had joined the old West Cornwall Railway during blasting operations in the new cutting below Camborne incline, they dug into the snow banks, shovelling to either side on the level stretches, and up into the wagons in the choked cuttings. It began to snow as they reached Praze, and the wind, which had increased to a brisk gale, continually caused new falls. Still they kept hard at it but not until 3 pm did they find Monday night's train in Polcrebbo cutting. After a meal break, and fortified by a large bowl of scalded milk provided by Mrs Rowe, they resumed shovelling, but an hour elapsed before the engine was freed from a 14ft drift. By then the storm was so bad that Clymo ordered a return to Gwinear; one extra passenger was carried, farmer Rowe, who travelled down to Praze to get food, as the side of pork which had fed his family and the railwaymen since Tuesday was almost finished.

More spadework was going on at the River Fal port of Devoran, where quay men and miners were discharging coal from the local collier *Erimus* which had come in on

Monday from Porthcawl, and whose sister the *Trefusis* had steamed up to Wales against the blizzard. Their coal normally went up Carnon valley on the small mineral line to tin mines around St Day and Scorrier, but the tracks were believed blocked in many places; indeed, early that morning auctioneer Thomas Gill of Falmouth, who was bound for Veryan, had twice gone into deep drifts near Carnon village, and after being rescued by the smith and several miners had abandoned both his courage and his journey.

However, one of the company's sturdy saddle tanks was coupled to half-a-dozen wagons filled with miners and quaymen, and went up the valley to investigate. The snow was deep around Baldhu, where two Truro workingmen, Henry Tippett and Charles Libby, had nearly suffocated in a drift on Monday night. Libby had been engaged by Doctor Whitely of Truro to take news of his father's death to the Rev Whitely of Baldhu, and he had persuaded Tippett to accompany him. They got within 100 yards of Baldhu church, then sank chin-deep in snow, and barely had strength to crawl to a nearby farm, where farmer Mitchell agreed to deliver their message. The two young men set off on the return to Truro but wandered into another drift and would have died had not some farmhands searching for sheep heard their cries and taken them to the farm of Mr Stephen Jose. They recovered sufficiently to leave at dawn; soon afterwards police constable Rickard of Devoran hobbled into the farmyard, having sprained both ankles by falling into the snow near Wheal Jane, and so exhausted that he too had to stay for several hours.

The white waste of the slopes of Carnmarth, where on Tuesday a Redruth man had made desperate but vain attempts to rescue his dying pony, finally brought the little tank engine and wagons to a halt in the driving snow, and ended hopes of bringing coal from Devoran. Neither could it come up from the opposite end of the line, as the deep incline cutting on Buller Hill was brim full. Around there it was so bad that provision waggons could not take the road to the mining village of Four Lanes, and at nearby Wheal Uny miners had to tunnel under the snow to the engine house. In Redruth town the surveyor's gangs were clearing Fore Street, but the only vehicles able to get around easily were the heavy brewery drays, hauled by two enormous Shires, and with a boy postilion riding the lead horse. Not even these could face the Porthtowan road, where only a narrow track could be opened up for pedestrians. At Treleigh, close to where the perishable goods train had been derailed, a lad named Julian had got lost while on his way home from Redruth on Monday night. His father and the police had searched for him in the blizzard until, in the early hours, he was discovered safely put to bed at Treleigh Farm.

Nowhere did Thursday's return of the blizzard strike harder than at sea, where many worn-out crews were nursing crippled ships towards harbour. One of them was the 91-ton *chassemarée Frère et Soeur* of Vannes, which had sailed from Swansea for Charlestown with 155 tons of coal, late on Monday afternoon. She lost her foremast off Morte Point and anchored until 4 pm on Tuesday, when Capt Constante Leguien cut away the wreckage and stood down Channel.

Without headsails the *chassemarée* could not hold her course, and at 1.30 pm on Thursday the NE gale drove her on to South Pelistry reef off St Mary's, Scilly. The five Frenchmen jumped overboard, but only the captain and his brother, the mate, sharing a lifebelt, reached Mount Todden, where they were helped ashore by farmer Owen Legge. By dusk the *Frère et Soeur*, which was owned by Capt Leguien and had been launched at Brillac near Vannes in 1869, had been battered to pieces.

At the same time as the *chassemarée* was being dashed on the Scilly rocks a crippled barque was sinking off the

Bishop rock. She was the 500-ton Dutchman *Magellan*, a week out from Shields to Santos with coal, and had been driven from the Downs on Monday night. Two steamers had ignored Capt Schapp's distress signals, but rescue came at 1 pm on Thursday with the Danish brig *Alexes*, Hansen master, fruit-laden from Messina to Copenhagen.

Already the 1,396-ton steel full-rigger *Senator Weber* of Helsingborg, five days out from Cardiff to Rio with coal and a crew of nineteen, had succumbed to the battering she had received between Lundy and Trevose. All her masts had come down in a tremendous squall, and for three days she was kept afloat only by constant pumping. A schooner appeared late on Wednesday and the Swedish chief officer and five men put off in a boat and caught up with her after a hard five-mile pull, finding that she was the Russian *Lojo* of Karis. Her master put about and ran down on the *Senator Weber*, but the ship's lights suddenly vanished as she capsized and sank, drowning the captain and twelve sailors.

By early Thursday afternoon the NE gale was almost as bad as Tuesday's; at Par a Breton sailing crabber stranded on the beach, but was later refloated. The storm did not prevent Capt McMillan of the Ayr steamer *Burnock* from towing the helpless *Stannington*, which had been adrift for sixty hours, into Falmouth. Behind them was the Liverpool coaster *Anglesey* towing the 885-ton iron barque *Firth of Lorne*, in ballast from Hamburg to Cardiff, which had lost her tug ten miles south-west of Lizard and had been on her beam ends since Tuesday. The Liverpool tug *Flying Dragon* came in to coal and reported losing the Glasgow clipper *Ellen Ballymore* off the Wolf when the towing hawser fouled her own propeller. Several schooners hove-to off Trefusis, among them the *J. A. Jackson*, one of whose crew, nineteen-year-old Alfred Miller, died as they entered Falmouth from exposure and injuries received during Monday night's blizzard.

On the South Devon coast the gale had upset an attempt to rescue the Duke of Edinburgh from Taunton by way of Torquay and the Admiralty paddle yacht *Vivid*. She came in from Devonport through heavy seas at noon, but conditions were still so bad on land that the Duke was unable to travel down, and eventually completed his journey by rail twenty-four hours later. At the same time as the paddler was thrashing across Torbay, the Brixham trawling ketch *Inter-Nos* encountered the ketch *Sunshine*, London to Exmouth with manure, about 25 miles south-east of Berry Head. The ketch had lost her mainsail, boats, bulwarks and water-cask, which had left her exhausted crew parched with thirst; the *Inter-Nos* towed her into Brixham that night for an agreed salvage award of £250.

Throughout the rest of Thursday afternoon the blizzard raged on but did not deter one Sennen shopkeeper. Taking advantage of road clearance around the village by seventy fishermen led by the Rev Isabell, he led seven donkeys in a string to St Just, where 'provisions were obtained, and the adventurous tradesman, followed by his donkeys—now laden with well-filled baskets—returned triumphant...' Nor did it prevent an old woman walking eight miles from

'... led seven donkeys in a string to St Just'

St Just to Penzance to ask for poor relief, which was not granted; though at St Agnes, where the storm had detained the relieving officer, the workhouse guardians paid the relief from their own pockets.

In Devon, workers on the Plymouth leat, which supplied the city with water from Dartmoor, battled on all afternoon, but at 5 pm the mammoth task had to be temporarily called off. The first warning of an impending crisis had come early on Tuesday, when Mr Bellamy, the borough surveyor, who had bitter memories of the 1881 blizzard, had stated that only 2,000 gallons, or two days' supply, remained in the Hartley reservoir. Next day, taking all available corporation staff, he had gone up to Head Weir, meeting on their way Mr Weekes on his trudge home from Horrabridge. The task of clearing the leat proved enormous; the mayor, Mr J. T. Bond, and other officials tramped through the snow up to Roborough to see how bad things were, and in answer to Mr Bellamy's plea for 200 men, he called a meeting of the Water Committee.

A local contractor offered 100 men but this was insufficient, and Mayor Bond appealed for help to General Sir Richard Harrison, KCB, commanding officer of the Plymouth garrison. As in 1881, the military responded promptly; 100 marines and 200 soldiers of the Welsh regiment were ordered out. This was fortunate as many of the contractor's men, on discovering that no food was provided, had flung down their shovels and gone home. Others, however, kept digging throughout the night, and shortly after dawn more labourers and troops, the Welshmen under Lts de la Chapelle and Ready, and the marines under Lts Mullins and Drake-Brockman, arrived by special train at Yelverton. They formed gangs and spread out along the leat, which in places lay under twelve feet of frozen snow.

The fresh snowfalls made the work doubly arduous, but the sweating marines and soldiers were supplied with food and 'at intervals with hot coffee' by the military commissariat. By late afternoon when work ceased one and a half miles had been opened up down to Yenadon, while the military had cleared far up towards Dousland, and near Roborough reservoir over three miles more of the leat had been freed of slush and ice. At 6 pm the wet and tired soldiers and marines shouldered their shovels and converged on Yelverton station, where they found the relief train, commanded by inspector Northcott, which had cleared the GWR branch line to Launceston that afternoon. When the train pulled out, 600 men were crammed into its twelve coaches for the run back to Plymouth. All went well until 7.30 pm, when it halted at a danger signal just outside Laira Junction. After a short delay the train rolled on, but the points were jammed and instead of going up the incline to Mutley the engines slewed off towards Friary station. With a crash of buffers they backed out again, but a light carriage owned by Mayor Bond was derailed. The Welsh soldiers in the next coach shouted a warning, but nobody heard and the engines increased speed. Mr Bellamy shouted to the signalman as they screeched past, and he gave the drivers a red light just in time. The soldiers jumped down into the snow, formed fours and marched away to Raglan Barracks, leaving Northcott's bone-weary breakdown gang to right the train; it was 10 pm before it came into Millbay station.

Meanwhile, yet another passenger train had been caught by the blizzard of Thursday afternoon. Double-headed by a pair of LSWR express engines, it had left Devonport Junction at 2.30 pm bound for all stations to Waterloo, and its subsequent fate is best told by one of the passengers, Mr Frederick Townshend.

He had left Exeter by a fast down express at 3.10 pm for Tavistock, to 'witness what a guard by the up-train from Plymouth described to me as one of the sights never to be seen again'. The weather looked bad from the outset of his journey, and abandoning the idea of reaching Tavistock, he alighted at Bridestowe station. Here he found enormous drifts; the short walk from the station to the Fox and Hounds Inn was blocked by snow four yards deep, which swallowed the hedges and weighed down the trees in the beech avenue. On Doe Tor there were 'mountains of snow', and it was so bad below the station that he decided not to go into Bridestowe. The landscape was certainly one of the sights he would never see again.

While waiting for a train back home he spoke to a local policeman and two stalwarts who arrived from the village with sacks to fetch loaves which his train had brought down from Okehampton. The policeman jokingly asked if he would like a 'tommy' (loaf) as he might be glad of it before the night was out; Bridestowe itself was on the verge of famine, and in a few hours would be again cut off by great snowdrifts. Eventually the 2.30 pm from Devonport Junction rolled in, several hours late, and Mr Townshend got one of the few spare seats and settled back, 'delighted with the grand impressions of snow on Dartmoor'.

But just beyond Sourton Church the train halted in the notorious 'Darkie's Cutting'; the guard reassured everyone that it was 'only a little snowdrift', but hours passed and they did not move, though

. . . the whistling of the engines seemed to remind the passengers that the officials had not forgotten them. Darkness soon followed, and we had no illuminant to render our hours of weariness passable beyond a few wax vestas. I invariably carry literature on my railway journeys, but my copy of Matthew Arnold's essays lay useless. To make ourselves comfortable for the night, as well as the circumstances admitted, was our only alternative; and so think of those at home who were listening for our footsteps. I believe the officials of the company did all they could to reach us from Okehampton, but the fearful elements baffled their persistent efforts. No one who has not experienced it can have any conception of the blinding effects of a Dartmoor snowstorm such as that which prevailed in that locality on Thursday night. The drifting snow soon enveloped our carriages, and we gave up all hope of escape until we were dug out. Our next object was to continually let down the window and brush away the snow, so as to make egress and air possible from that source.[1]

A loaf of bread was brought along for each compartment, and the resourceful Mr Townshend produced whisky and eggs, which he beat up together and passed around. Soon after daybreak some more bread and some ham arrived, but

...there was no cessation of the drifting snow, and I buoyed up the hopes of my fellow passengers with the opinion that until ten or eleven o'clock I feared there was no hope of its discontinuance. The cold throughout the night was intense, and it was not until the engine drivers came to our carriage and offered to fill our foot-warmers with hot water, that our ... (situation) became bearable. The welcome voice of Superintendent Medway I recognised about half-past ten: he, with his large staff of workmen, having been trying to liberate us. It did not take me many seconds after we were free to leap out of our carriage window ... The view of our snowed-up train as we left it cannot easily be forgotten. We walked 300 yards to reach the engine and tender, to take a few passengers back to Okehampton, prior to sending another to those who were left. We passed another train on the down line that had been snowed-up since Monday ... The grotesque appearance of the blue-jackets who occupied seats on the coal in the tender of our engine, required an artist to hand down to posterity.[2]

It was late afternoon before the rest of the passengers,

including the women, were rescued from the train, which was buried almost to the carriage roofs; some of them tramped through the snow back to Lydford, the rest waited for the relief train to come out again from Okehampton.

The sleeting dawn of Friday 13 March brought more trouble on the Cornish main line, when the 6.25 am up train left Penzance in Stygian gloom and ploughed into a new and deep drift in a cutting above Angarrack viaduct. Assistant guard Uren walked back down the line to protect the rear of the train, while the engine was uncoupled and steamed up to Gwinear Road, where a down mail was waiting. Her engine joined the other and they went down to Angarrack and extricated the stranded train, which eventually reached Plymouth only forty minutes late.

At Millbay, breakfast had been ready from an early hour in expectation of the arrival of the breakdown crews from Ivybridge. They had crawled out of their snow-covered trains at daylight to find the drifts that had built up during Thursday's blizzard even worse than they had feared. The carriages of Monday night's up mail posed a serious problem, as they had been derailed and damaged by the collision; rather than waste precious time, Compton had them tipped down the embankment, a drastic though effective way of clearing the main line. Towards noon the relief train started out for Plymouth headed by the pilot engine and snow plough; coupled behind her came the powerful express engine, the dead engine of Monday night's mail, and two vans packed with gangers. They negotiated several drifts but on the way down Hemerdon Bank the pilot nosed into a snow block fifteen feet deep and 400 yards long. Wearily the men shovelled the rails clear once more, and finally, at 3 pm, they arrived at Millbay station for their breakfast. The refreshment-room manager had been warned ten minutes before, and so was prepared for the famished horde that poured across the platform. Wet and tired, all, including Mr Compton and the Swindon officials, filthy with mud and soot, they ate their first meal in nearly twenty hours, half loaves of bread and hunks of ham and roast beef, washed down by great mugs of scalding tea and cocoa.

For the first time in ninety-two hours the GWR main line between Plymouth and Totnes was open, at least sufficiently for a makeshift timetable to be organised. The 'Zulu' express came into Millbay at 8.30 pm, complete with guard, drivers and one or two passengers who had stuck it to the bitter end. At 10.40 pm the first up express since Monday night left Millbay for Paddington.

Friday evening also saw the final disaster of the blizzard at sea, which cost more lives than had the wreck of the *Bay of Panama*. At 9 pm, 140 miles south-west of the Bishop rock, the 1,222-ton iron screw steamer *Roxburgh Castle* of Newcastle, ten hours out from Newport to Pireas, reeled heavily to starboard in a shower of sparks and a rending of plates as the 1,428-ton Nourse clipper *British Peer*, Dakin master, Calcutta for Queenstown via Trinidad, sliced into her just abaft the funnel. The steamer settled very fast, and though her crew of twenty-two pulled away in the starboard boat, it was sucked down as she foundered, only eight minutes after the collision. Capt Tryer, a native of Brixham, removed his jacket and boots and swam through heavy seas until rescued by the *British Peer's* quarter boat. Other men were heard shouting in the water, but could not be found in the darkness, and only one other survivor, an able seaman, was picked up.

The *British Peer* was herself in serious trouble, as her bowsprit, jibboom and headgear had gone, and only the fore bulkhead kept her afloat. Nevertheless Capt Dakin remained in the area for several hours, vainly searching for more survivors, and the crippled ship was eventually taken in tow 90 miles south-west of the Wolf rock by the collier *Morglay*, Cardiff for Marseilles, which brought her up to the Manacles, where the Falmouth tug *Triton* took over. It was a pretty piece of salvage, which brought Capt Hughes and the crew of the *Morglay* £2,000 at an Admiralty salvage court in June 1891.

Before Friday night was out, the last epic solo journey of the blizzard was completed, when police constable Greenslade, who had left Southpool on Wednesday to fetch the county coroner to hold an inquest on the dead from the Start wrecks, reached Newton Abbot by train. He had travelled to Kingsbridge by steam launch, and at 4.30 pm on Wednesday set out across the snowbound fields, reaching the California Inn late that night. The people left by Capt Angel were still in residence, and the constable joined them for the rest of the night. Next morning he reached Kingsbridge Road station, but as no trains were running he trudged on up the line, extremely hungry as the landlord of the station hotel had nothing to spare. That night he sheltered in a signalbox, and on Friday morning walked to Totnes, where, as the railway lines were clear, he was able to complete the last few miles of his journey that evening in relative comfort. On the return home, constable Greenslade took a train to Kingswear for Dartmouth, but then had to walk to Southpool, where he arrived on Saturday night after an absence of four days.

9

Aftermath at sea

Saturday 14 March, the fifth and last day of the great storm, came wet and cold, but the wind had at last hauled westward and later in the day gleams of sunshine broke through and the air felt a little warmer. The sea still ran very high, but at 7 am the long-lost *Seuvia* hove to off Plymouth breakwater. She had ridden out Monday night's hurricane, and next morning sighted a disabled schooner. Capt Ludwig readied a lifeboat, but just then the London collier *Arondyck* appeared; she ignored the schooner and made for the crippled *Seuvia*, and not until the captain had refused aid several times did she cease steaming around the liner and go to the distressed vessel. Both drifted away into the snow, and though Capt Ludwig believed the *Arondyck* had sent across a boat, he greatly feared that the schooner (which was never certainly identified) had sunk with all hands.

Help for the *Seuvia* herself came on Wednesday morning from the 1,393-ton London steamer *Acme*, which was too short of coal to attempt a tow but brought the liner's chief officer into Falmouth. Travelling on the newly opened branch line to Truro, he reached Plymouth at midnight and alerted the Hamburg-Amerika agents in London and Southampton, who each sent out a tug. The Admiralty had no suitable tug at Devonport, so he put off with the GWR tender *Smeaton*, which rolled violently in Thursday afternoon's gale. She had still not sighted the *Seuvia* when, very short of coal, she had to put into Falmouth, where, for the second time in forty-eight hours, the distracted German caught the train to Plymouth.

Meanwhile the *Seuvia's* engineers had, after considerable labour, got the engines working again twenty-five miles south-west of St Agnes, Scilly. She then managed to reach Plymouth to the great relief of the agents, though her passengers had taken things in their stride; 'We had faith in our captain, and faith in our ship.'[1]

Falmouth Roads were packed with ships, large and small, which had entered in varying states of distress. The damaged Glasgow dredger *Manche* reported seeing a barque off Lundy flying distress flags, but could give no help in the mountainous seas. The tug *Rosetta* brought in the 650-ton composite barque *Shun Lee*, Cardiff to Acapulco, which lost her cutwater and jibboom in collision with the Liverpool clipper *Lota* off Scilly, and the disabled 1,595-ton steamer *Ville de Pernambuco* of Bayonne came in under tow of the *Black Cock*. Thomas Law's iron clipper *Morayshire* was so badly damaged that even after repairs her crew refused to sail her. From the Blue Funnel liner *Horrex* to the little Caernarvon schooner *Ellen*, vessels took shelter in the roadstead. On Sunday men of a score of nationalities gathered at the Royal Cornwall Sailors' Home for a service of thanksgiving.

About the time the *Seuvia's* welcome siren was wailing

Page 155

(above) *Villagers in the blocked streets of Bude on Wednesday;* (below) *The aban-doned mail cart', a contemporary artist's view of an incident of the blizzard in Devon*

Page 156

Coastguards act as bearers and guard of honour at the funeral of lifeboatmen and seamen drowned at Dunge-ness on the night of Monday, 9 March 1891

outside the breakwater at Plymouth, the smallest salvage prize of the blizzard was picked up 233 miles south-west of Scilly, when the Shaw Savill clipper *Astrea* sighted the 70-ton Bude ketch *Ant*, with her ensign inverted. She had left Sandersfoot on 4 March with coal for home, but was blown far off course by the blizzard. Capt Hines and the mate, exhausted and frostbitten, lay huddled in the folds of the mainsail; the thirteen-year-old cabin boy, nephew of the owner, Capt Stapleton of Bude, had died of exposure and been buried over the side. The two men were brought back to the *Astrea*, and chief officer Moore and seaman Philpotts brought the *Ant* into Plymouth on Monday morning.

Even before the storm died it was apparent that the small sailing coasters had suffered tragically, though some shared the *Ant's* luck. Like her, the 69-ton Truro schooner *Ulelia* was blown far out into the Atlantic, and reappeared just as hope for Capt Benjamin Phillips and his crew was being given up. Off Sennen, the crew of the Penzance schooner *Secret*, expecting every moment to be wrecked, cowered as avalanches of snow fell from the rigging, and Capt Harvey of the schooner *Integrity* was forced to slip and run between the Longships and Land's End, when he found his anchor chain sawing down through the bows.

Another West Country coaster, the 70-ton ketch *Francis Beddoe* of Appledore, salt-laden from Sharpness to Gloucester, was driven down the Bristol Channel. When she got into a fearsome tide-rip both Capt William Slade and mate Philip Quance reckoned they were off the southern tip of Lundy, but dared not hoist sail, and throughout Monday night remained hove-to on the starboard tack. The third hand and Quance, who was not a robust man, took to the cabin completely exhausted, leaving Capt Slade to work the ketch alone.

He lit the navigation lights but as he was unable to put

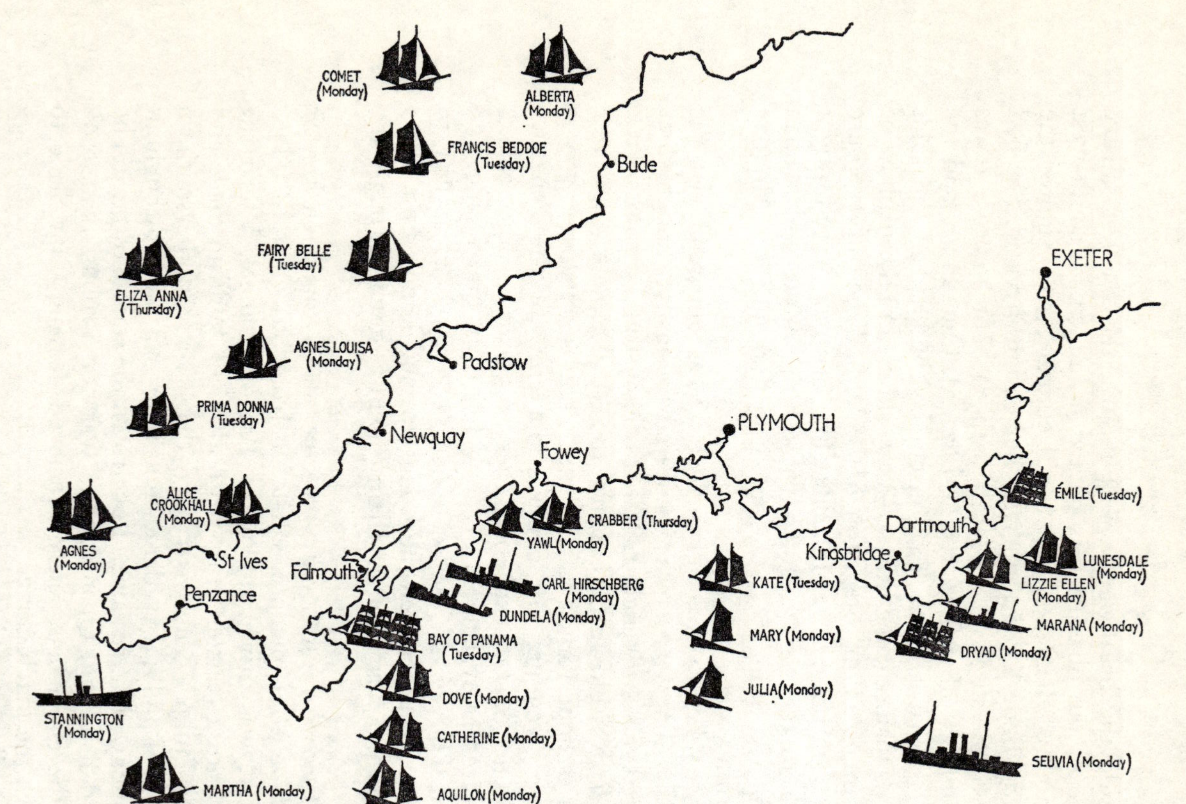

Shipping casualties around the coast of Cornwall and Devon during the blizzard week

158

them in their proper place the *Francis Beddoe* was in danger of being run down and he was afraid to go to sleep. Wednesday's sunshine came as a tremendous relief, but in the early hours of Thursday, the green glare of a starboard light appeared over the ketch. Desperately Capt Slade waved his red port light, but closer loomed a big full-rigger going down Channel under foretopsails; then she rushed by, her wash filling the lee decks. He fell to his knees and gave thanks, though some hours later came another near disaster, when the fore scuttle broke away, but he managed to nail some canvas over the hole.

Eventually he put the ketch on the port tack, lashed the helm so she would head-reach slowly, and staggered down to the cabin, rubbing himself and his crew with paraffin before climbing into his bunk. Some hours later he woke, stiff with cramp, to find the *Francis Beddoe* pitching along off Godrevy light. By this time they were all sufficiently revived to work the sails, and Capt Slade headed for home, where he and his haggard crew found that they had been given up as lost and arrangements made for the care of the crew's dependents.

Another escape saga became known when the schooner *Fanny* of Beaumaris, Bangor to Bremen with slates, limped into Hayle on Sunday morning. She landed the crew of the 110-ton Yarmouth schooner *Stanley*, which had left Hall Quay, Yarmouth, almost three weeks previously for Cardiff with bagged flour. She raised the flash of the Longships light during Monday evening's hurricane after a voyage bedevilled by calms and fogs. Just after dark the main topmast staysail flogged itself to ribbons. As Tuesday's dawn slowly lightened the whirling snow, Capt Pearson went down to the cabin to light a fire and brew some coffee, but only minutes later an enormous sea thundered across the decks. When the *Stanley* came up the boy cook (later Capt) W. J. Beckitt, who had just taken over the helm from the able seaman, found himself flat on his back, clutching the two bottom spokes of the wheel, having been somersaulted right over it. The first thing he saw was the top half of the wheel bobbing away astern, and then Capt Pearson's head emerging through a torrent of water still pouring down the companion; the able seaman lay against the booby hatch clutching an injured shoulder.

The *Stanley* was so shattered, on deck and aloft, that it was astonishing that she did not sink there and then. But she was leaking badly, and Wednesday morning's bright sunshine found the crew still baling and pumping forty miles south-west of Scilly. When another schooner was sighted they decided to abandon ship, but before they could do so Capt Pearson had to repair the punt, using two oilskin frocks, sennit and large-headed copper nails. They launched the craft through the broken port gangway, baling as they pulled away from the sinking *Stanley*, and drifted seven miles before the *Fanny* was able to bear down and rescue them shortly before their punt slipped beneath the waves.

The *Fanny* herself was in no spruce condition, and the *Stanley's* crew were welcome hands, particularly during Thursday's ENE gale, and both rescued and rescuers were almost too tired to stand when a pilot took the *Fanny* into Hayle. They were lodged at the Steam Packet Hotel, which had only just been vacated by the crew of the *Alice Crookhall*.

Anxiety for news of menfolk at sea was increased by the absence of the mail and telegraph service, and at Port Isaac 'after three days, some of the wives collected £1 (a large sum when husbands' wages were £3 10s or £4 a month with big families to keep) and got a man to walk to Wadebridge post office, eight miles by road. When he got to the top of Church Hill, which was not too bad, not a hedge or a road could be seen, so he went straight across country and got there in less than six miles'.

Two of the Padstow fleet, which had many Port Isaac men in its crews, were missing. The 102-ton ketch *Fairy Belle*, launched at Newquay in 1872 for the celebrated 'Fairy' fleet of Capt W. B. Williams, had sailed from Cardiff on 8 March for Par, but vanished off Trevose. Another ketch, the *Comet*, which was insured with a Padstow club for £500, had left Newport on the same day, coal-laden for Mevagissey, and was last seen off Hartland on Tuesday morning. On board were Capt Charles Harvey, only just married, mate Reuben Prior of Port Isaac, who left a wife and four young children, and able seaman Henry Irons, unmarried.

Port Isaac was already in mourning for Capt Anthony Wills, one of the many village sailors trading to the Cornish clay ports. He had been drowned early on Monday morning when his ketch *Alberta*, two days out of Par for Gloucester, had foundered off Lundy. Able seaman Tom Barron of Mevagissey and mate John Wills, the captain's brother, were rescued by a steamer and landed at Barry, but Capt Wills was the sole support of their aged mother at Port Isaac.

At Penzance, hope lingered for the *Prima Donna* for many more days, but the next edition of the Penzance parish magazine noted sadly the 'loss of five of our brethren in the town, three of whom lived in our parish, who were drowned at sea'. A fund for the five widows and nineteen orphans, the youngest only eighteen months old, was started by Mayor Mitchell, who donated £5; ten St Just miners in the Kimberley diamond fields sent £10, and the sum collected eventually reached several hundred pounds.

Penzance was also the port of call of the schooner *Eliza Anna*, inward bound from Caernarvon with potatoes for Mr Lovell, which failed to round Land's End during Thursday afternoon's gale. Also still missing was the Bude ketch *Agnes*, which had been launched by Stapleton of Bude in 1878, and carried a crew of four. Odds and ends of wreckage drifted ashore for weeks after the blizzard; the nameboard of another missing ketch, the *Agnes Louisa* of Newquay, came ashore at Scilly, as did the sternboard from the longboat of the *Prima Donna*. On 16 March another tragedy was confirmed when the hulk of the Plymouth trawler *Mary Jane*, one of the fleet which left Sutton harbour on the Monday morning, was found on the Scilly rocks; she had been crewed by three men and a boy.

The inevitable sequel to the disasters around Start Point came with the inquest on 15 March at the London Inn, Hallsands, when only two of eight sailors from the *Dryad* were identified; seventeen-year-old apprentice Alfred Ford of Hull, whose father had journeyed to Devon, and William Irvine, sailmaker of Shields, who had a cork foot. The *Dryad*, launched by T. Roydon of Liverpool in 1874 as an iron clipper, had been a flyer in her day, but had recently been cut back to a barque. Evidently a Tyne pilot, who had been dropped off Beachy Head at 9 pm on Monday, had warned Capt Thomas that his compass was several points out, but the barque was still under a strong press of sail when she struck the Start cliffs.

While the last of the *Dryad's* men was being buried at Stokenham on Monday morning, an inquest was being held on those washed in from the sunken *Marana*, all of whom except the young second officer, Newbray Hall, had been in the big lifeboat with Nielsen. Hall, whose father was chief solicitor to the LSWR, was the only one recovered from the captain's jollyboat.

This was not quite the end of the story of the wrecks at Start Point; on 25 March Nicholas Rundel, molecatcher of East Prawle, discovered in a field below the coastguard station the oilskin-clad body of another Swedish fireman lying face down in a melted drift. By an evil quirk of fate he lay on the opposite side of the hedge around the field where Rasmussen had died, otherwise signalman Perry and the coastguards might have found him. He was buried two days later, his 'coffin ... covered by the Union Jack, fishermen of the village acting as bearers, whilst a large number of people accompanied the body to Chivelstone.'[2]

The heroism of those who risked or lost their lives for others did not go unrecognised. The RNLI committee on 12 March voted £500 to a fund for the dependents of the coastguards drowned at Dungeness, and the rest of the lifeboat crew were awarded double pay. Further awards went to the crews of St Agnes (Scilly), Brixham and Falmouth lifeboats, and £2 to the head launcher of Penzance lifeboat, who contracted pneumonia after wading around in the bitterly cold water. The six Beesands fishermen who saved the survivors from the *Lizzie Ellen* received £1 each, and the Board of Trade presented skipper Gempton of the smack *Gratitude* with a rosewood binocular case for his rescue of the *Crusader's* crew. On 7 April Joseph Hendy James was given a purse of money on behalf of Lloyd's in appreciation of his epic journey to Falmouth, which had left him suffering from rheumatism.

Monetary reward of another sort came to W. H. Lean of Falmouth, who undertook to refloat the stranded *Carl Hirschberg* for £1,500. She lay so far up the rocks that he decided to 'launch' her down wooden ways, but first the reef which protected her from the worst of the seas had to be removed. Due to the proximity of cottages and the Independent chapel, blasting was dangerous, and so, reinforced by local fishermen and sailors, seventy salvage hands spent five weeks cutting a channel through the rocks, only to find that when the steamer floated she drew more water than they had expected. Worse still, on 23 April, just after a wooden cradle had been built under the bilges, a hard ENE gale drove the salvors back to Portloe, and heavy seas came with the spring tides. Meanwhile forty hydraulic jacks had been gathered from all over Britain and using these to manoeuvre the *Carl Hirschberg*, Mr Lean was able to refloat her on 9 May with the aid of Falmouth tugs

Pendennis and *Emperor* and to the accompaniment of cheers from hundreds of spectators on the cliffs.

After the blizzard the Porthoustock fishermen had come under attack when, on 19 March, the Rev Flynn, vicar of Mawnan, wrote to the papers accusing the lifeboat crew of cowardice during the wrecks off St Keverne on the Monday afternoon, and reviving the bitter argument as to whether the sailor on the *Bay of Panama* had been alive when the rocket line was cut. Some people sided with him, but he was rebuked by the Rev Mallach, rector of Ruan Minor and Hon Sec of the Lizard lifeboat, and the RNLI's own inspector found that the Porthoustock men, especially James Cliff, had behaved with considerable gallantry.

At the official Board of Trade inquiry held at the Coverack coastguard house on 14 May 1891 there were some heated exchanges, but the outcome was a general acceptance of the opinions expressed by chief officer Gibson and his men, and by Dr Leverton-Spry, who had attended the survivors and examined the bodies after they had been brought ashore. The sailors were dead when the Coverack LSA company arrived, and had probably been so for several hours. The charges against the lifeboat crew were also dismissed, particular importance being attached to the evidence of quartermaster McKetterick and able seaman Magnus Thompson that 'no lifeboat that had ever been built could have floated that night'. By the time the inquiry, which both praised and vindicated coastguards and lifeboatmen, had ended, it was evident that the Rev Flynn's charges were based solely on hearsay, collected mainly on the Wednesday evening from one or two fishermen who still believed that living sailors had been left on board the wrecked jute clipper.

The salvage of the *Bay of Panama*'s jute cargo became an epic in itself, and from April to October 1891 Porthallow Cove reverberated to the roar and rattle of steam winches. After inspection of the wreck by owners' and underwriters' agents, tenders were invited for salvage of the jute, and that of Captains Baker and Anderson was accepted. Henry Anderson, a Liverpool diver, had been working on the wreck of the Glasgow ship *Port Chalmers* on nearby Lowlands Point, and he was to lay the foundations of his Western Marine Salvage Co with his work below Nare Head.

Operations began on 24 March, and the salvors faced an arduous and dangerous task from the outset. At low tide they could just get around the *Bay of Panama's* bows in a rowing boat, but a long, jagged ledge lay astern. Amidships she rested on sand, and the jute bales were clearly visible through the rents in her hull. Most of the bulwarks had gone, and even a slightly rough sea slopped over the decks, which canted heavily seaward and were ankle deep in a mixture of sand, seaweed, fragments of canvas and thousands of ship's biscuits washed out from the gutted poop cabin.

After an auction of stores, lights, anchors etc, on 16 April which fetched good prices, the job began of clearing debris from around the holds. James Cliff and William Hill were soon employed, together with many other covers, and they were on board when Capt Anderson, a sturdy moustached figure in tweeds and bowler, blasted away the listing fore and main masts and a vast tangle of spars, chains and rigging. A buckled watertight bulkhead under the foc's'le head which kept the holds brim full even at low water was also dynamited.

The steam lighter *Concorde* of Penzance and the Falmouth tug *Lizard* were used to ferry out to Nare Head gangs of fifty men, who loaded the jute into the Truro barges *Maggie* and *Bessie Ellen*, with the clipper's own donkey engine working the fore hold and a temporary engine rigged above the main hold. Another steam lighter, a cranky craft which on 8 May was blown far up the Helford river and had to be retrieved by the *Lizard*, used her own derrick to top the after hatch. In the flooded lower holds Anderson and Baker donned their diving suits, a Falmouth diver being hired to work the after hold.

Bad weather added to the difficulty of their task and by the seventh week of salvage only 264 bales had been raised. Capt Anderson was confident that they could do better, and on 17 May alone 189 bales were discharged. Soon the men were working two tides, and in their scant rest periods slept in an old derelict house at Porthallow which became known as the 'Wreckers' Roost'.

But tragedy had not yet finished with the *Bay of Panama*. When work began just after daybreak on 5 August 1891, a large number of bales were waiting to be unloaded before the flooding spring tide covered the decks. Driving the midships donkey engine were George 'Sequah' Biford, a young Somerset labourer who had left the show of a travelling Yankee quack doctor named Sequah to join the salvage crew, and Henry Rusden, trainee mining engineer and youngest son of George Rusden, tug owner of Falmouth. Neither young man was qualified for the job, and perhaps they raised too much steam in their haste to clear away the bales.

At 4 am, just as James Cliff strolled aft from drying his clothes at the boiler, there came a violent explosion, which shook Porthallow village. Thirty salvage hands on the poop dropped flat as iron boiler plates and burning coal swept the decks like grapeshot. Cliff evaded all but a few cinders down his neck. Benjamin Price, who lodged with Biford, stood unharmed in the caboose surrounded by broken mugs of tea, but Henry Rusden was hurled through the carpenter's shop door and lay badly scalded, his leg fractured by flying iron. His father sprawled inert in a pool of steaming water, also injured, but 'Sequah' Biford had taken the full force of the explosion and been flung from the main hatch to the foc's'le head. Terribly burnt, he was rushed to Falmouth by the tug *Lizard*, but never regained consciousness and died at the Sailors' Home next day. The violence of the explosion was such that only the base of the boiler was left, and fragments were picked up in meadows half a mile away.

At a Board of Trade inquiry held at Falmouth the court discovered that the safety valve had been tampered with, allowing the boiler to work at too high a pressure, and the engine had already been overstrained in freeing the packed jute bales in the main hold. As the machinery was second-hand the true facts were never elucidated, but Capt Anderson was ordered to pay £70 court costs.

By October 1891 only about 500 bales remained in the *Bay of Panama's* hulk, and then came a succession of easterly gales which finally broke her up, and also drove the St Malo brig *Buron* under nearby cliffs. Today, only the legend of the great jute clipper survives, though her bell still hangs in the belfry of a small chapel of ease at Bosahan, on the Helford river, only a few miles from where the *Bay of Panama* met her doom on that bitter March morning in 1891.

10
Thaw

Although the seas soon calmed and most crippled ships reached port, on land the effects of the 'unwelcome guest' remained for weeks, even months. The thaw which set in during Saturday was hastened by showers of heavy rain and a warm westerly wind, but throughout the weekend the struggle to open the roads and get mails and food through continued as before. The main railway lines were almost back to normal by Saturday evening, though gangers still hacked at the great snowbanks poised above the LSWR metals around Meldon, and the GWR between Ivybridge and Brent. Both companies had lost heavily; the GWR revenues for 9–16 March were down nearly £13,000, and the LSWR £3,662, 'all but £650 of which was lost from the non-conveyance of passengers and parcels.'

There was also the great cost of clearing the lines, wages of the scores of extra labourers employed in the shovel gangs, and repairs to snowed-up rolling stock and damaged engines.

On the branch lines, which were vital to the country districts of Cornwall and Devon, it was ten days before normal services could be restored. The engine and coach from Princetown lay rusting in Eggworthy cutting for a week, and on the surrounding moors the roads were only cleared after immense labour by convict gangs. (Picture, p 52.) One Dartmoor woman whose sailor husband was away at sea was imprisoned in her home until neighbours cleared the door; she passed on to her children an amusing illustration of the depth of the snow, in the dialect words of a young man from her childhood home of Ilsington, near Haytor. Visiting her just after the blizzard he said, 'You knaw ole Mother Ball—you knaw 'ow tall her is dawn ee? Well her got lost in the snaw, so that'll tell ee.'

The first contact Princetown had with the rest of Devon was on Saturday afternoon, when postmaster Tooker, accompanied by a postman and a prison officer, trudged into Yelverton Junction. Awaiting them there were twenty-five bags of mail, fourteen of which and some newspapers they took back with them, and 'were received with much enthusiasm'.

Saturday also found water once more flowing along the Plymouth leat after another prolonged battle against snow and ice. Thursday's blizzard added another three feet to the drifts; on Friday morning a special train taking 300 labourers and 300 soldiers and marines up to Yelverton was blocked at Bickleigh station, and conditions were then so bad that all the military and fifty other men were sent back to Plymouth. The rest went on to Yelverton and after sheltering in a barn until the storm eased set to work again on the leat. By 7 pm a clear passage for water existed along its whole ten miles. A hundred volunteers remained to work on until a good stream was running, while the rest returned to Plymouth with Mayor Bond by a special train at 9 pm. The lessons of the past week, added to his knowledge of the chronic water famine caused by the 1881 blizzard, were not lost on Mr Bond, who was later to play a leading part in the construction of the great reservoir at Burrator.

The Devonport leat was also blocked with frozen snow fifteen feet deep, and in one place by a fallen tree fourteen feet in girth. One of the men working on this leat noted that the gangs had 'nothing hot to drink after they left home until they returned in the evening, and that their food froze in their pockets'. But thanks to the unstinting work put in on both leats there was no serious water shortage, though many people had to resort to borrowing. Standpipes erected at various points helped the situation, as did 'Messrs Polkinghorne, at their brewery in Bedford Street, Messrs Dunniford & Son, mineral water manufacturers of Russel Street, and Mr Lewis, aerated water manufacturer of Athenaeum Street, (who) supplied hundreds of the inhabitants, free of charge, from their artesian wells.'[2]

In Cornwall, success had also finally crowned the efforts of the Gwinear Road gangers who at dawn on Saturday, and aided by a further eighty men from the main line, tackled the largest drift on the branch, at Prospidneck. It was 400 yards long and fifteen feet deep, and lay 'curled and twisted into fantastic shapes, rolled over like huge travelling rugs, pinnacled like a series of mountain tops in miniature, or sticking out bold and jagged like cliffs on a seashore. Tree boughs were swathed with radiant garments of white, great clots of glittering ice patched the sides of neighbouring hills.'[3] By noon a way had been cut through, and superintendent John Peach, one of the most energetic officials organising the clearance of the railway lines, decided to run a special train laden with papers and mail.

Men and shovels were taken on board, and the train was quickly between the walls of snow, the sides of white, scraped by the footboards, giving out a hissing sound like the escape of steam from the sides of an ocean steamer. The engine threw up snow in clouds of glistening spray, and glided along the slippery rails with a slow and cautious pace. In a minute or two there was a shout of 'She's through!'[4]

At 12.35 pm the first train since Monday night reached Helston, and superintendent Peach addressed the men from a luggage trolley. He thanked them for their labours and, after three hearty cheers, the 150 gangers, William Clymo amongst them, marched four abreast to their dinner in the town.

Two hours later a score of bedraggled figures plodded into Helston, pulling a farm cart piled with mailbags, the load of a four-horse waggonette which had left Penryn station at eight that morning, with a man at each bridle and six others shovelling. At Rame village they encountered an enormous drift, and even a gang of navvies who joined them failed to dig through, so each man shouldered a mailbag and they waded four miles until they managed to borrow a cart. As no horses were available they laid hold of the shafts and, pulling and pushing, set off for Helston. They were the first people to get through from Falmouth, though a Mr Berryman had followed the road in the other direction on Wednesday, a few hours behind James Hendy James. He rode out of Helston with some letters but, like James, had to leave his pony and finish on foot.

The borough surveyor's gangs were busy on Saturday as the roads around Helston had been particularly bad. One resident, William Henry Trewin, late coming from work at the height of the storm, had been found by his family

... in the deep snow frozen stiff, when they brought him in the house we all thought he was dead but through our rubbing and the warmth he came around and helped himself ... Next morning we were all snowed in, could not see through our windows or open our door until my stepfather, mother and stepbrother worked very hard, and I remember the snow came into the kitchen and they got shovel and pick to clear it.[5]

Falmouth was slowly returning to normal, and the branch line to Truro, which had remained open despite Thursday's blizzard, brought a torrent of delayed mails and parcels. The shipping agents were also very relieved when, at five o'clock on Saturday evening, the telegraph to Truro was restored, though only by a single wire, as throughout the week urgent business messages had been sent to London via the French, Spanish and American cables. At the other end of the single wire, Truro post office was also overwhelmed. Forty large baskets of mail awaited sorting; so heavy was the traffic that thirty extra staff had to be sent down from Plymouth, and over a thousand messages were despatched.

Drifts still affected the roads out of Truro, and on Sunday evening the Rev Thompson, who had taken morning service at Chacewater, lost his cab near Treliske and had to trudge some way before he was rescued by a passing carriage. Sunday service was also affected at the miners' chapel at Tregajorran, under Carn Brea, when that evening's preacher, Capt Josiah Thomas, having shovelled his way out of his Tregenna Lane home at Camborne, found he could get no further than Bassett Road. At Broadhempston in Devon, too, some of the congregation walked to church along the top of the hedges. A young minister given shelter on a farm near Ruan High Lanes put dignity aside and was to be seen amusing the children by playing snowballs, wearing a suit several sizes too big which the farmer had lent him to replace his own wet clothes.

The country roads were deep in slush and snow, but tradesmen, carriers and householders set out to fetch food and fuel. Near Kingsbridge, a Mrs Cubitt and two friends used a horse-drawn sleigh to cross the snow to the town. Bogged down at Borough Corner, they walked on into Kingsbridge and ordered supplies for East Allington, which Mr Grills, the sleigh driver, picked up after making a long detour across country. Most of the roads were too bad even for a sleigh, and barge-loads of provisions were towed down the estuary to Hope Cove and Frogmore by the steam launch *Nautilus*. More supplies were taken to Southpool and East Portlemouth by the steam launch *Lively*, which had also been bringing the mail up from Salcombe since Wednesday. In Cornwall, a small steamer from Penzance was used to land food for the fishermen of Penberth and Porthgwarra on the beach at Porthcurno.

During Saturday evening Paul's horse bus belatedly arrived at Penzance from Germoe, and in its wheeltracks followed Osborne's bus, which had been stuck at Breague since Monday evening. In the deep snow around that village was found the body of sixty-year-old Eliza Mitchell, who with her brother, Jack 'Figgy' Mitchell, led a vagrant life, eked out by taking in washing. She had left home to buy coal on Monday evening, but had fallen into a deep drift near Wheal Vor mine.

Up on the high moors of West Penwith, waggons had at last succeeded in reaching St Just, where scores of hungry miners and Sennen fishermen waited with sacks and handcarts. The coast roads were even worse, and a man who brought herrings from St Ives on Monday was snowbound in St Just with his donkey cart for seven days. By the end of the week many such 'lost' travellers had returned, including Mr Clemo and his stepbrother, of Clemo's horse bus, which had been buried to its roof at Mount Ambrose, outside Redruth. The owner purchased a bottle of whisky to sustain him and spent the night in his bus, while his companion took the horses into Redruth, walking in several circles before finding the main road again.

Abandoned waggons and their loads were beginning to be recovered throughout the West Country, though it was to be days before normal trade could be resumed. Not all firms were as businesslike and obliging as the Devon butcher who sent three men to walk six miles in the raging blizzard, which took them from 8 am to 6 pm, for the satisfaction of knowing that one of his most important customers was 'thoroughly grateful...for his kind thought'.

In North Cornwall contact was being made with difficulty by the end of the week. On Friday afternoon Camelford regained touch with the outside world when 'four persons on horseback, unrecognisable from the quantity of snow that covered them, entered the town in single file.[6] They were Mr George Martyn, manager of the North Cornwall Coach Co, his chief clerk, and the guard and driver of Monday night's coach. Mr Martyn, who had done the same relief journey from Wadebridge in a dog-cart during the 1881 blizzard, reported that the road, though blocked in places by eight feet of snow, might be made passable. The town clerk at once organised a shovel gang, but it was four days before the coach could return to its normal service between Launceston and Wadebridge.

The heavy drifting all around Camelford and the surrounding villages had claimed hundreds of sheep, and also farmer John Kinsman, the contractor for the mails from the little sub-post office at Otterham church. The postmistress, Mrs Tucker, had sorted the letters, and he had sent his farm boy to take the bag. The boy returned a little later, saying he could not face the storm, and forty-year-old Kinsman, a strong man, declared 'If you can't, I can!' and took the bag. Their path

...lay over the Downs, a wild open moorland stretch which cut off a mile or so from the road to Camelford. They eventually got there and delivered the post, and set off back...After a while they saw a light about half a mile away but did not know where they were. Farmer Kinsman had become quite exhausted and lay down by a hedge, telling the boy to go on and...bring help. The boy wrapped his coat about the man and left him. The farm turned out to be Halgarden Farm, and (he) got help and retraced his footsteps in the snow to find farmer Kinsman. When they got there, however, he was dead from cold and exposure.[7]

Most of the schools closed down for the blizzard week, due to an almost total lack of pupils, for those were the days when children from five years old walked upwards of three and four miles, twice a day, for their weekly 2d worth of education. Many children were not even immured at home but, marooned en route from school on Monday, were looked after for the week by other parents in the open-hearted way of country dwellers.

One small girl who walked home from the church school at Camelford was detained by her friend's mother, and 'the children then had to stay in their bedroom because the snow was as high as the window and the pump house and back kitchen were full of lambing ewes'. Her elder sister was looking after their grandfather at Pencarrow Advent, where drifts were also level with the bedroom windows, and she 'had to make a clearing with the fire shovel, or make muffs of two cake tins and push it away in that style, so as to be able to shout to neighbours'.

Two young brothers, Alfred and Ernest Jasper, who lived at an isolated farmstead near the foot of Roughtor, walked three miles to Camelford each day to school. That Monday they set off to trudge home through the snow with a friend, Bill Bennett, but at Gillings they were called in by a Mrs Piper and told that they were not to go on until someone came to fetch them.

A little later the young Jaspers' father came searching for them. Ernest Jasper and Bill Bennett were down in the back kitchen seated in a big old-fashioned settle, watching the fire blaze up with each gust of wind and pretending it was a blacksmith's forge. Unfortunately, as young Bennett was sitting inside, Mr Jasper only saw Ernest peeping round the end of the settle when he looked in and next morning a distraught Mrs Bennett, without news of her son's whereabouts, arrived at Gillings completely exhausted, after crossing the moor in snow so deep that at Aldermoor she walked over a buried gate. The boys had to stay indoors all that day, 'watching the snow falling and blowing, from the window'.

The blizzard had also stopped work in the slate quarries around nearby Delabole, and many quarrymen went abroad to dig out sheep and cattle. A Mr Burnard, who lived in the village, had a little terrier dog which marked the snow wherever the sheep were buried, a service many West Country dogs rendered their masters that Wednesday. Thomas Greenwood, who farmed Delabole Barton, which was owned by the Delabole Slate Co, had 300 sheep buried. The men 'made a hole in the hedge of the field and lifted the sheep out into the road, hoping to get them in the waggon house in the yard, but the sheep could not face the blinding snow and were all buried'. Mr Greenwood also lost three valuable colts, and 400 fowls which could not be got in and 'all froze to death, lying all over the yard.' On Monday he had sent three teams of horses to Bodmin Road station with slate, but on returning they ran into a great bar of snow at Helland Bridge and had to stay there all night. A horse in one of the teams froze to death standing up. They got the others into a farm, but it was some days before the three drivers, John Cross, Thomas

Scone and Jack Cloke, could get back to Delabole. Another man who lost his horse in the same district was Isaac Mutton, a smallholder near Delabole; he ran into a drift on the way home and had to leave the horse, which died before it could be dug out.

The neighbouring small port of Boscastle had also been cut off for a week, and it seemed another would pass before the mail cart could get through from Camelford, but the village store was well stocked, so the villagers settled down to await rescue. Mail was brought to the village by Mr Mark Olde, who made the journey from Boscastle to Camelford station and back walking on the hedges all the way, apart from crossroads where he rolled himself across.

Conditions up on Bodmin Moor were just as bad as they had been throughout the week. At Mount Warleggan, seven miles from Bodmin,

> ... the pumps were all frozen and the running water also from the spring ... they had to melt the snow to make tea, also to make meals for the family. They boiled a piece of dried pork and such vegetables as potatoes and turnips that they had indoors and also boiled suet puddings. Neighbours who lived near Carburrow Tor went over the moors searching for sheep buried, they found them by little round holes in the snow, and travelled over fields and moors with horse and cart digging them out. They said you could not see the hedges. In places the snow drifted from eight to ten feet.[8]

One moorland child who was always to remember the great blizzard lived on a holding called Butters Tor at the foot of Brown Willy, the highest hill in Cornwall. He and his father were returning with one of their cows from a neighbouring farm; the snow was so blinding that even the cow could hardly face it, but she led the way home, with the boy holding tight to his father's coat. Next morning they could not see out of the windows and had to dig their way to the farmyard to get at the housed animals. They 'could not see any roads, gates, hedges or rivers, everything was all frozen hard . . . There was an awful loss of sheep and ponies as they had got buried alive'.

Most of the inhabitants of bleak Bodmin Moor were ready to fend for themselves, even at the end of the winter. They 'used to buy a bushel of flour, and a wooden bucket of lard with a cover, which was then called "grease". They killed their own pig and made their butter and cream'. It is doubtful whether the average household today could contend so well with a siege; in the words of another blizzard veteran, 'People then used to talk about being "snowed in", they usually had enough food in the house to last several days, not like today when they live from day to day'.

Blizzard or no blizzard, people were born or married or died. In Cornwall, one intrepid midwife gathered up her long, heavy skirts and cloak to walk six miles along the hedgetops to deliver a baby girl. In Bradoc parish another nurse, Mrs Anna Harris, took to the broad back of a hefty farm horse, lent her by the squire of Boconnoc, and set out accompanied by a Mr Henry Burt on another to carry out her duties. For her services during the blizzard the parishioners and others presented her with a marble clock with the inscription: 'Presented to Nurse Harris by numerous friends, for her devoted services during the blizzard 1891'.

With similar determination Charles Tucker of Lapford married Mary Dicker of Throwleigh, even though the snow 'was hedges high and had to be shovelled away before they could reach the church.' Another bridegroom, rather than give best to the weather, reversed the usual order of wedding ceremonies. He was on board the 'Dutchman' express which came off the rails at Camborne but managed to reach Penzance on a breakdown train in time for his marriage to Miss Polly Blewett on Tuesday afternoon. Finding that his brother, thinking it impossible for him to arrive, had postponed the ceremony, the groom ordered the reception to be carried on, and the customary dance was held in the evening. The wedding took place quietly the next morning.

Funerals presented a more serious problem and there were many instances of the coffin being carried on men's shoulders across country. A Mr Hayne, who died at Camelford, was brought for burial at Davidstow in this way, the bearers walking on the top of the hedges with telegraph poles for their guide. Usually, however, funerals had to be postponed because it was impossible to reach the parish church and cemetery. A man who died at Port Navas reputedly could not be buried at Constantine for three weeks, and the coffin of a Marazion man who died in London was held on the blocked railway from Tuesday until Saturday.

One of those who died during the blizzard was Amelia Michell, at her son's house in the Outlands Woods, not far from Bodmin.

> She was to be buried at St Neot where the family had resided for many years. The cortege started out on what in those days would be a long journey. Conditions eventually became so bad that the horses could not go on any further, so a few miles outside Bodmin the hearse and carriages were left by the wayside and the funeral abandoned; the mourners and horses struggled home through Arctic conditions. The old lady lying snug in her coffin was left in the deserted hearse. The undertaker said to her grief-stricken son 'Never you fret, Sir. This weather she'll keep as fresh as a daisy until we can come to bury her proper.'[9]

One of the subjects uppermost in everybody's mind, after the anxiety for food and warmth, was mail, particularly as these were the days when husbands and sons were away for months at sea, or working in the American mines and the South African goldfields. It was a week before letters began to move as the branch lines were opened up, and even longer before mail vans were on the road again. There was no traffic on the Plymouth road between Ivybridge and Modbury, or the mail route from Totnes, until 19 March, and daily papers still had to come by sea to Dartmouth. On 17 March Foale's bus was hauled from its sodden resting-place near the California Inn, and on 25 March the first coach since the Monday night of the blizzard left Kingsbridge for Kingsbridge Road station, splashing through deep and muddy pools left by the melting snow.

In Totnes the snow cleared from the roads was heaped shoulder-high along the pavements, but the indefatigable postmaster, Mr Heath, set out with two high tandem carts to get the mail through to Kingsbridge. At Halwell they had to leave the vehicles and continue on horseback, 'obliged to leave the main road for narrow lanes and cross fields, the horses plunging through snowdrifts higher than the hedges, then jumping from the hedges again into the main road.' On the way they discovered an abandoned mail van which had left Kingsbridge on Monday night, and soon after that they took to a narrow trench which had been dug in an earlier attempt to get the mail out, where 'the snow wall on each side of them was in some places higher than their shoulders, although on horseback.'

They arrived at Kingsbridge at 2.30 pm, and half an hour later Mr Saunders, the driver of the Dartmouth coach, drove into the town with a cob and trap, accompanied by its owner Mr Cross of Strete, having summoned volunteers to help them on the way by blowing a rousing coaching horn. He had already been active over the weekend catering for the hunger for newspapers; none had reached Kingsbridge or Salcombe for the week, and many people who were disappointed when the crew of the packet steamer *Express* forgot to bring any from Plymouth were soon offering a shilling a copy for the *Western Morning News*. On Friday evening the *Kingsbridge Journal* and the *Salcombe Gazette* had appeared, only half their usual size, but were quickly sold out.

Also on Saturday afternoon the week's copies of the *Western Morning News* reached Rose Arundell's home at Lifton, and

... at last Weevil and Dyer came with more mail, but still on horseback, letters written on the 12th but none from Plymouth way, only on Sunday morning did we get those, and dated 10th; also one from Wilmot from Broadwindsor with various postmarks—Beaminster 13th, Bridport 13th, Dorchester 12th, Exeter 14th, Okehampton 14th, Lifton 15th.

They (the postmen) went off again Saturday afternoon with letters from here and returned Sunday morning and off again in the afternoon, but not yet can 'wheels' reach Bridestowe. At Stowford they were pretty deeply snowed in. Northey's men started for there with a load of coals for the Rectory. Reached Lew Down but found a block, so sent sacks on men's backs, and left the rest in someone's shed for the night. The men from the rectory dug out a good part of the snow and tried to get the donkey cart up the hill for the rest of the coal, but at last abandoned that and had wheelbarrows and sacks.

Jordan the coachman managed to walk here from Stowford on Thursday with a note from Aunty to enquire for us. We three, Papa, Mama and I, each wrote back our accounts of the storm and other items. It was quite a pleasure to write again.

On the 18th Rose Arundell was out walking again, and found 'a way cut for vehicles—some of the cuttings were far above my head ... I had to walk over the snow as high as the hedge and some places I sunk in above my knees, but it was fairly hard so that it would bear.' She ends her account with an observation from the *Western Morning News* that 'there were avenues and woods looking as if some mighty machine had swept right through and crushed everything in its passage, leaving only the young and pliant able to rise again.'

The loss of sheep and lambs had been enormous. Almost every farmer in Cornwall and Devon lost between 10 and 100, and at Bigbury nearly 400 died on one farm, many of them blown over the cliffs into the sea. Mr S. Square of Thurlestone lost over 100 valuable sheep and lambs, and in the Modbury district alone the casualty list was over 1,000. In some cases lambs were dug out from beside dead ewes, and one farmer found himself 'endeavouring to keep alive forty young lambs which had lost their mothers.' At Kingston and Holberton sheep were blown into the river Erme; one farmer who lost his whole flock and nearly all his apple trees said 'he could buy more sheep but he would not be able to get any fruit-bearing trees in his lifetime, it was his cider he was worried about.'

Even on the somewhat sheltered banks of the Tamar there was 'great havoc among the fruit trees. Mr E. Elliott, of Landulph, lost about three hundred apple trees, many of which had been planted by himself thirty years before.' Mr James of the Passage Inn lost fifty-six cherry and apple trees. Behind a barn in his orchard two geese had been sitting on twenty-two eggs, but

> ... the barn having been badly knocked about, and the whole orchard in a state of wreck, the fate of the geese was not held in much doubt ... the snow being cleared from the back of the barn, however, the geese were found still sitting in the same position as that in which they had last been seen. With the exception that they had evidently worked their heads about, keeping the cavities large enough to give them breathing room, it

was quite clear that they had not attempted to move. Warm food and hay were at once given to them, and ... in due course, eleven goslings were hatched from the twenty-two eggs upon which the parent geese had sat through such a trying time.[10]

There were numerous instances of lambs being born under the snow, and some of the ewes blown over the river cliffs lodged there and gave birth to lambs 'like little goats about the cliff'. At Redlap Farm, near Stoke Fleming, a lamb was dug out of a drift unharmed after being buried for sixteen days, and at Beer Barton Farm, Bere Ferrers, they not only survived being buried but also apparently thrived on being dosed with gin intended to warm them. Even after several days the greater part of most flocks was dug out alive. Indications of the buried sheep were small holes in the snow, or a translucent patch where the surface had dampened with the warmth of their bodies. Many of the farmers, like Mr Jasper of Poldue, found the ewes by prodding with a long stick. The two boys watched their father dig down until he found one, then climb down into the pit to lift it out, and saw 'the little cave it had made, its breath having melted the surrounding snow, and it had picked away at the grass around it.'

On 29 March a lad trudging towards Elston in East Allington parish fell through the snow into a small cavern, out of which scrambled a ewe, unharmed after twenty days. There were sheep on Exmoor reputedly rescued after upwards of six weeks, and even in the sheltered fields around Gulval in West Cornwall an 8ft drift held two rams alive until Sunday the 15th.

Comparatively few horses were lost, most being stabled, though some young working colts out at grass and harnessed horses left in drifts died. The vast majority of horses on the road not only survived but frequently saved their masters' lives too, by finding the way home, though one cob in South Devon made his driver's struggle worse by repeatedly turning his tail to the blizzard rather than face it. On higher land even cattle were lost, and a number of donkeys and ponies died, though one prize donkey was dug out of a drift at Wheal Buller, near Redruth, alive after nine days. Of the moor ponies there is little record, as people then had less interest in their fate, but deaths, particularly of the foals, must have been many. On Bodmin Moor the dry February had caused serious fires, and with the ensuing blizzard the ponies had no grass for many weeks. Even so, when the thaw came and the new grass began to grow, they made a remarkable recovery. One man who lived out there said he had never seen ponies 'go ahead' so quickly in his life.

It was fortunate that the fine weather had advanced the corn and potato planting, as no more seed could be got in until May. The crops already in the ground were not much damaged by the blizzard, although the prolonged frost and the cold April weather retarded their growth and spring flowers lasted well into June. Among the worst hit by the storm was the daffodil harvest in the Scillies. At St Winnow, corn drilled just before the blizzard without time to harrow it in germinated beneath the snow and at the thaw was found to be three inches high.

One couple beat the blizzard by planting their potatoes in spite of the threatening sky. Soon

> ... the snow began to fall and the neighbours laughed. Mother and Dad were snow-covered before the job was finished. Needless to say the crop was the best ever. Then Mother and Dad could laugh, as the neighbours were so late in planting their crops were poor. 'He that observeth the wind shall not sow; and he that regardeth the clouds shall not reap.'[11]

Another man who acted quickly on the approach of the snow employed extra hands to pull his turnips and greens, and when at length he was able to get them to Plymouth market he made a handsome profit.

The thaw brought its own perils as the moorland streams and rivers, swollen by tons of melted snow, caused serious flooding. The western counties were a quagmire. On Bodmin Moor the 'hills were gushing down like rivers', and the Tamar rose almost to the top of the arches of the bridge at Gunnislake. An old man who used to row daily across the river to oil the waterwheel at Wheal Russell mine, had to be rescued from the bedroom window of the island house at Weir Head. The wheel, which was 'his pride and joy', was carved in replica on his tombstone when he died.

But for masons, glaziers, carpenters, paper-hangers and sawyers the blizzard was a literal windfall when the immense task of clearing up began. In the miserable east winds of March and April they took to their ladders to repair the countless broken windows, fallen chimneys and ruined furnishings. Hundreds of glass and even slate roofs had caved in beneath the weight or been stripped by the gale, and many that appeared unharmed were so damaged that when the snow thawed the slates and laths slid off too. Signs of the destruction were still apparent throughout the year, and it was many seasons before the woodlands recovered even a little of their former beauty.

On Good Friday a train-load of excursionists went to Plymouth from Penzance. The weather was cold, sleeting and windy, and the Dartmoor hills were still blanketed in snow. A young girl, looking for primroses on the sheltered banks of the Dart, found snowdrifts there late in April. Sheep-shearing at Wellshead was always on the second Tuesday in June, and on that day in 1891 snow still lay in the coombe opposite the farm. In Watern Coombe, Longstonne Bottom and Tavy Cleave, which was said to have been filled to a depth of 300 feet, it was high summer before the remnants of the drifts disappeared. Even in West

Cornwall the hills were white until May. Midsummer Day came and went, and the harvesters worked with scythe and horse team amid the scent of hay, while the snow of the great blizzard still lay on the ground.

APPENDIX: WEATHER CHARTS

Charts show isobars in millibars at 4 millibar intervals.

Fronts:

        warm
        cold
        occluded

Spot winds with arrows indicating wind force; one full length barb = 2 Beaufort numbers, $\frac{1}{2}$ barb = 1 force.

        = force 1
        = force 3
        = force 6

With some of the winds air temperature in degrees Fahrenheit is shown. Time of the charts is 0800 hours GMT.

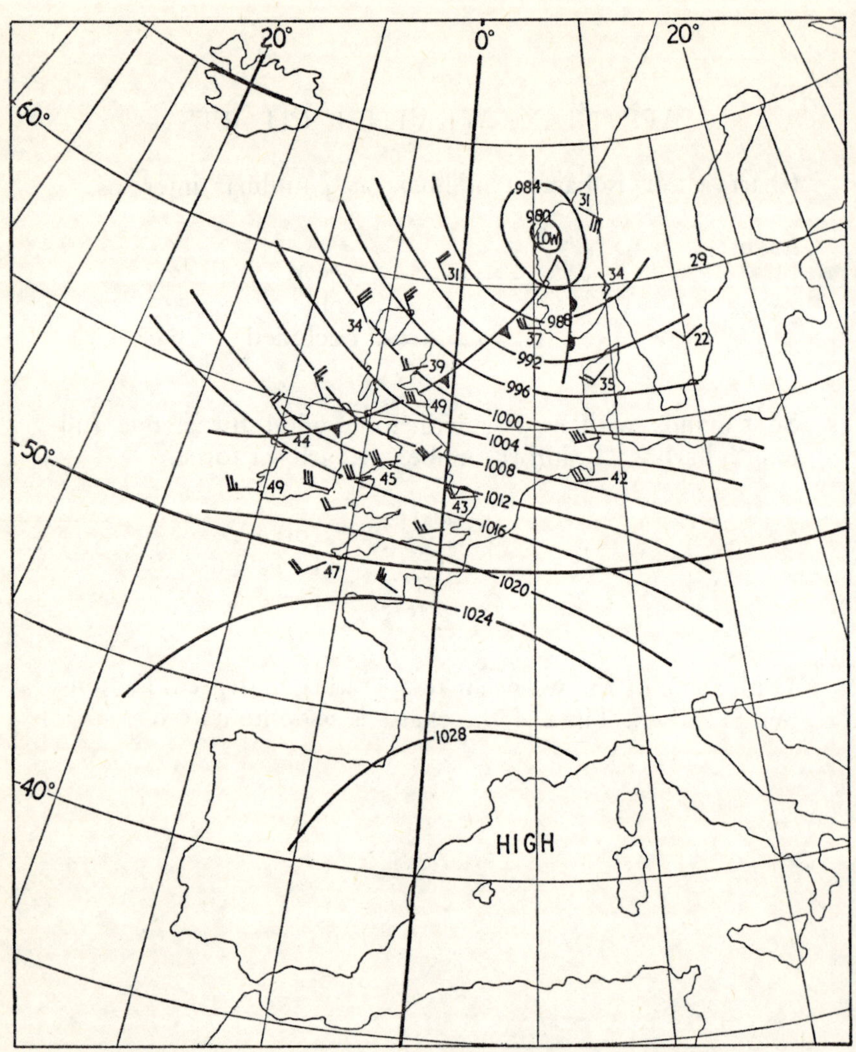

1.   6 March 1891. A deep depression has crossed Scandinavia and its associated cold front is making progress southwards across the British Isles.

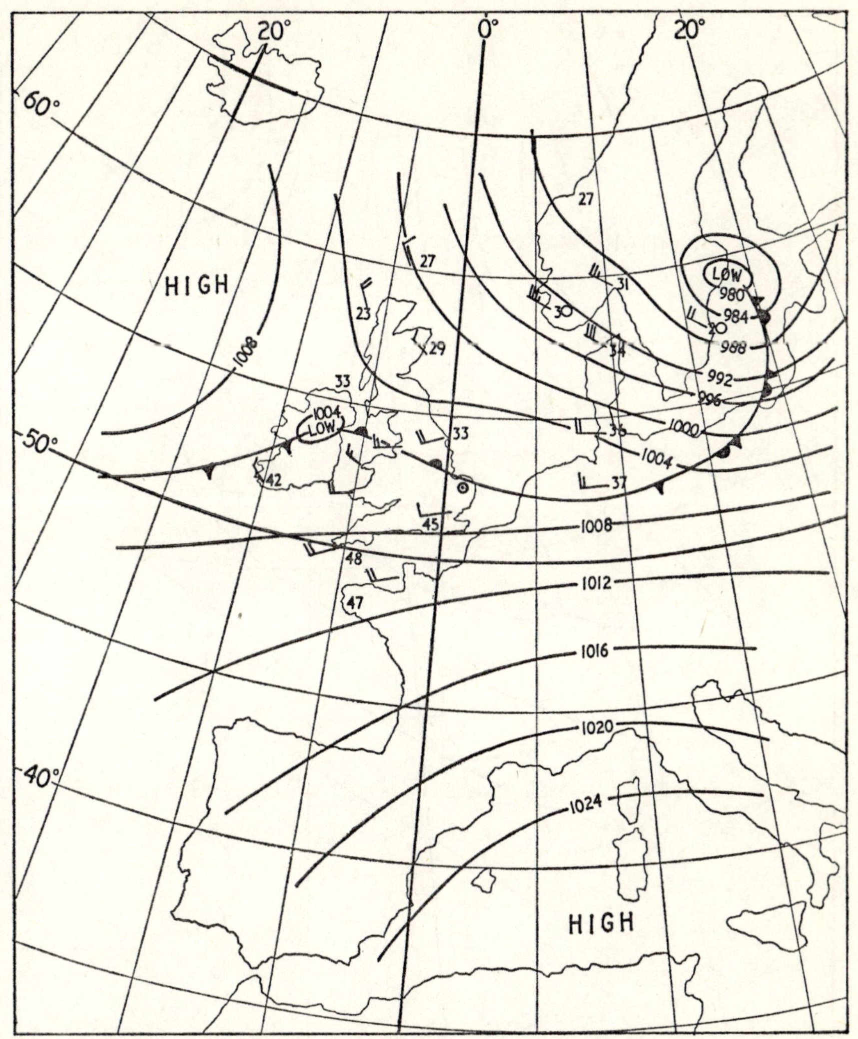

2. 7 March 1891. The cold front is waving and a secondary depression is forming over Ireland.

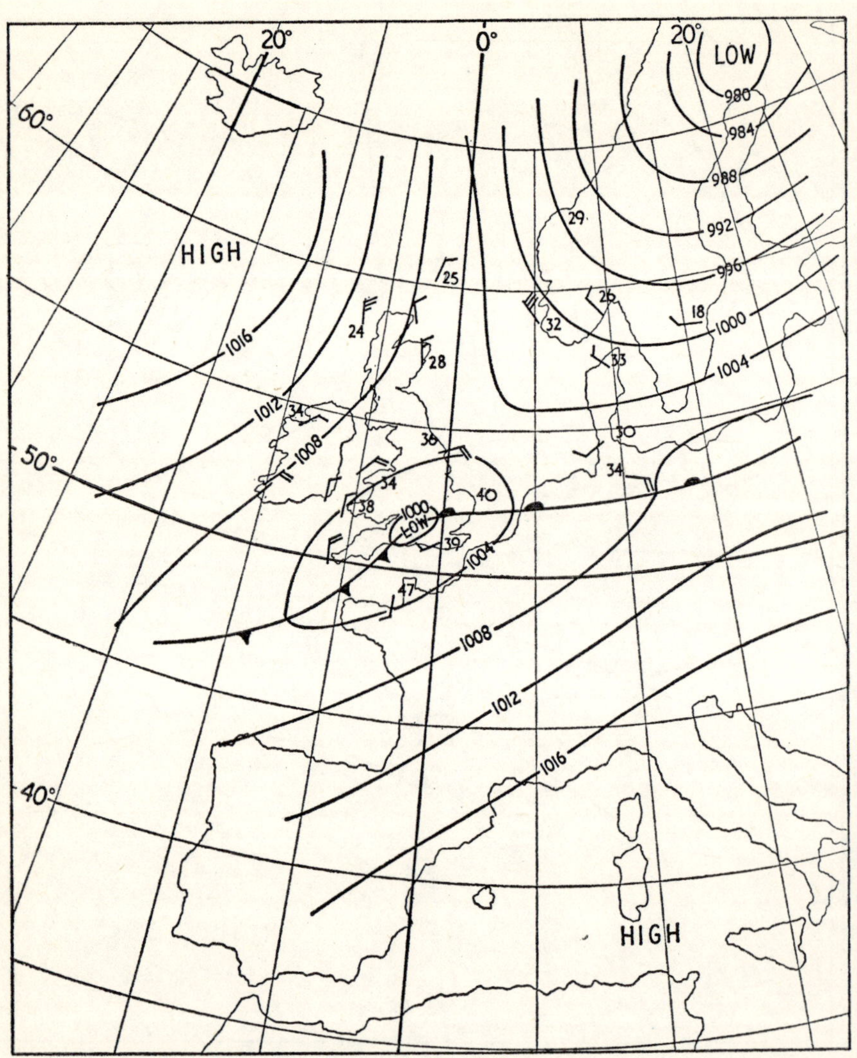

3.   8 March 1891. The cold front has moved well south of Lat 50° to the west of Britain, and the secondary depression is passing over the south-west peninsula, causing frequent rain.

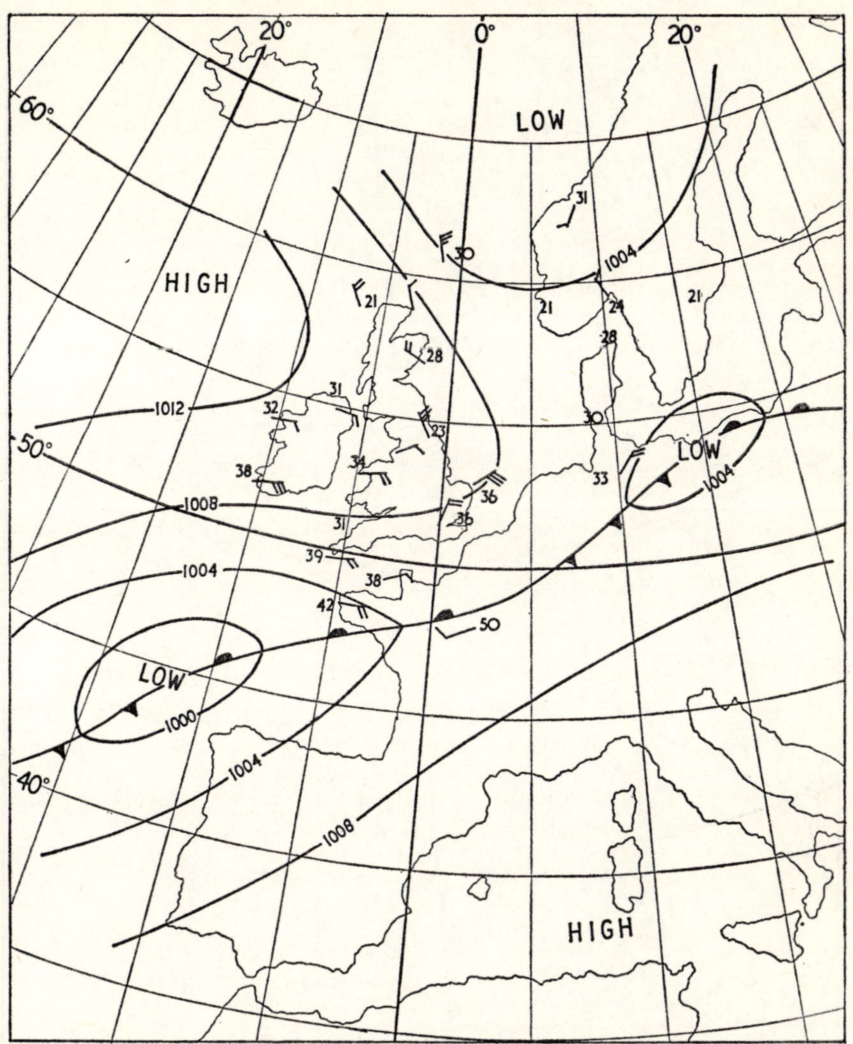

4.   9 March 1891. The secondary depression has moved east and a new depression is approaching Britain from the south-west, while ridges of high pressure close in on the British Isles from the north-west and the south-east.

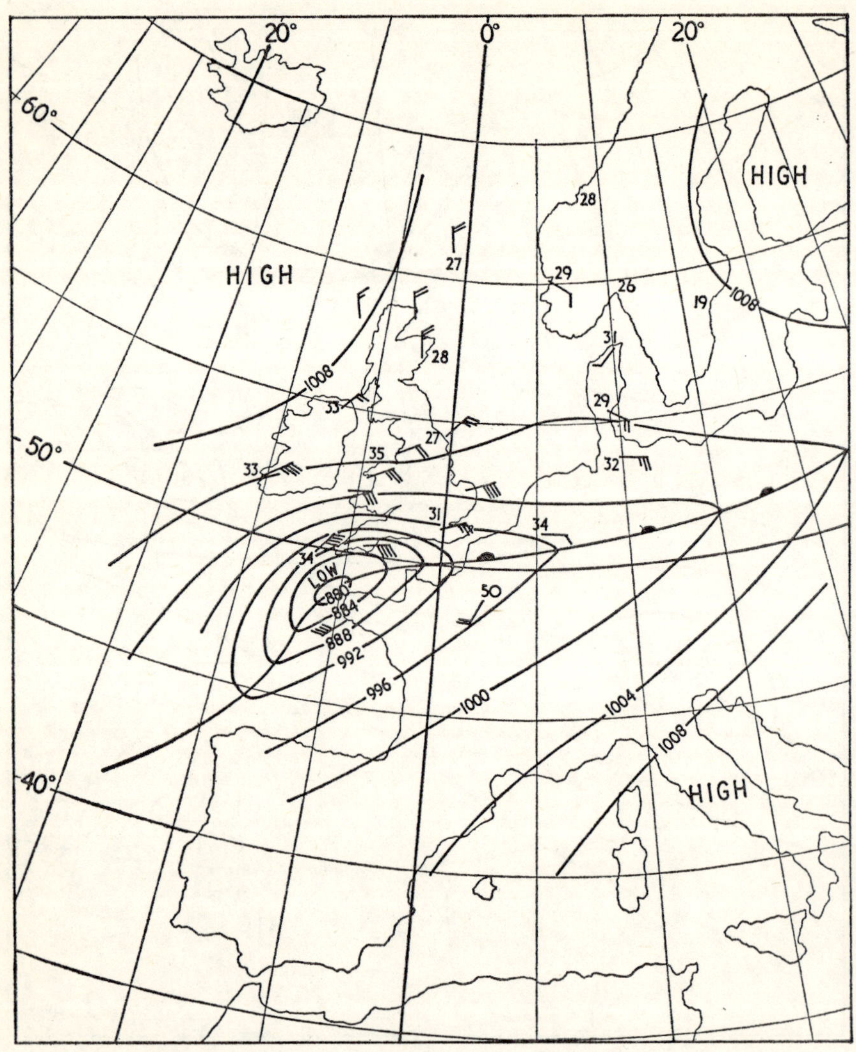

5.   10 March 1891. A third ridge of high pressure has appeared
over Scandinavia and the depression has deepened dramatically
over the south-west approaches.

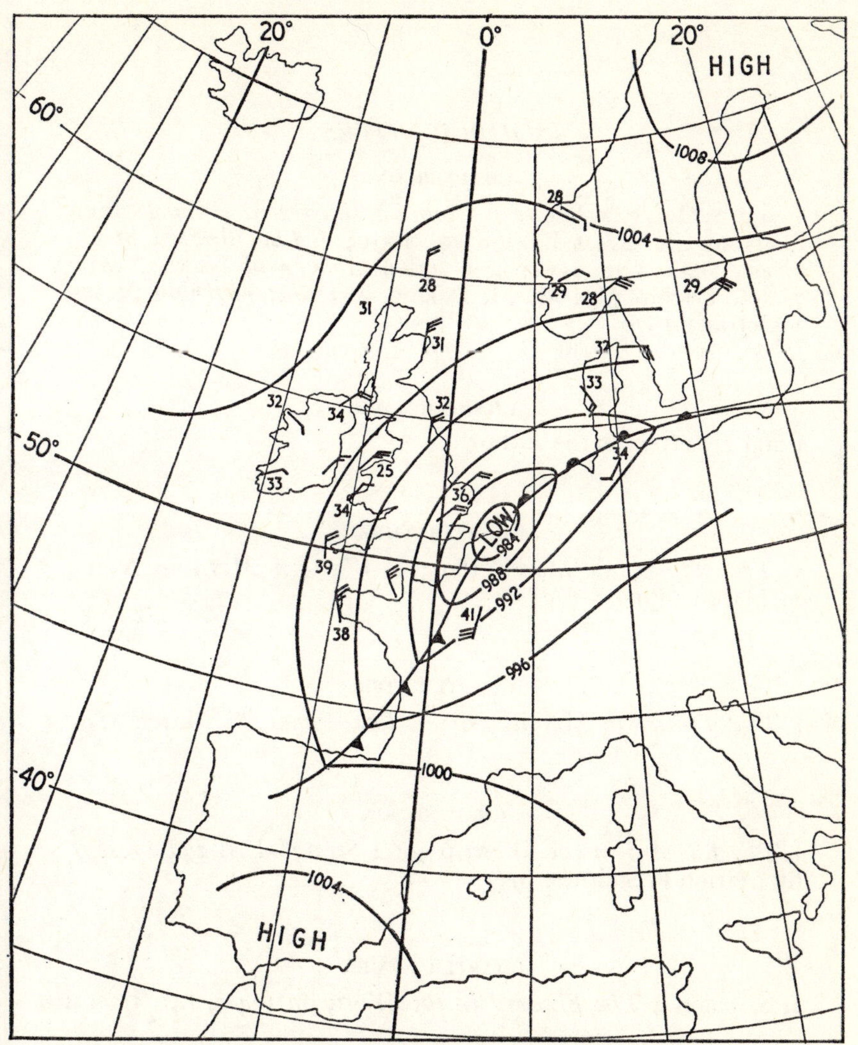

6.   11 March 1891. The depression fills and moves eastwards, and the worst of the blizzard passes.

SOURCE NOTES

CHAPTER ONE

1 and 2 *Doidge's Western Counties Illustrated Annual*, 'Incidents of the Great Blizzard of 1891'; 3 *The Blizzard in the West*, Devonport 1891; 4, 5 and 6 *Gallery of Nature*, 1846; 7 Letter from Mrs M. M. LeDuc, *Western Morning News*, 1 October 1970

CHAPTER TWO

1 and 2 Letters to the author

CHAPTER THREE

1 *The Times*, 14 March 1891; 2 *Western Morning News*, 11 March 1891

CHAPTER FOUR

1 *The Times*, 12 March 1891; 2 *The Times*, 11 March 1891

CHAPTER SIX

1 *The Blizzard in the West*, p 96; 2 *Strete—Past and Present*, by Marion F. Smithes, 1933

CHAPTER SEVEN

1, 2, 3 and 4 *The Blizzard in the West*, pp 134-5, 141, 10, 12;

CHAPTER EIGHT

1 and 2 As quoted, *Doidge's Annual*, pp 385-6

194

Source notes

CHAPTER NINE

1 *The Times*, 16 March 1891; 2 *Blizzard in the South Hams*, p 37

CHAPTER TEN

1 *Original Cornish Poems* by Wm Quintrell, Plymouth 1911; 2 *Blizzard in the West*, p 156; 3 and 4 *The Cornishman* 19 March 1891; 5 Letters to the author; 6 *Blizzard in the West* p 94; 7, 8, 9 and 11, Letters to the author; 10 *Blizzard in the West*, pp 88-9

BIBLIOGRAPHY

Athill, Robin. *The Somerset and Dorset Junction Railway.* David & Charles, 1967.

Bucknall, Rixon. *Boat Trains and Channel Packets.* Vincent Stewart, 1964.

Carter, Clive. *Cornish Shipwrecks: The North Coast.* David & Charles, 1970.

Carter, E. F. *The Railway Encyclopaedia.* Harold Starke, 1963.

Chandler, George. *Liverpool Shipping: A Short History.* Phoenix House, 1960.

Clinker, C. R. *The Railways of Cornwall: 1809–1963.* David & Charles, 1963.

Dawson, Maj. A. J. *Britain's Lifeboats.* Hodder & Stoughton, 1923.

Domville-Fife, C. W. *Epics of the Square-Rigged Ships.* Seeley, Service, 1958.

Ellis, Hamilton. *The South Western Railway.* Allen & Unwin, 1962.

Greenhill, Basil. *The Merchant Schooners,* Vols I and II. David & Charles, 1968.

Hamilton Jenkin, A. K. *Cornwall and its People.* Dent, 1945.

Haydon, A. L. *The Book of the Lifeboat.* Pilgrim Press, 1909.

Hughill, Stan. *Sailortowns of the World.* Routledge & Kegan Paul, 1967.

Kidner, R. W. *The Southern Railway*. Oakwood Press, 1968.

Knight, F. A. and L. M. *Devonshire*. Cambridge University Press, 1910.

Langmaid, Capt K., DSC, RN. *The Sea Thine Enemy*. Jarrolds, 1966.

Larn, Richard, and Carter, Clive. *Cornish Shipwrecks: The South Coast*. David & Charles, 1969.

Lubbock, Basil. *The Coolie Ships and Oil Sailers*. Brown, Son & Ferguson, 1955.

Lubbock, Basil. *The Last of the Windjammers*, Vols I and II. Brown, Son & Ferguson, 1963.

Macdermot, E. T. *History of the Great Western Railway*, Vols I and II. Paddington, 1931.

Michell, F. *Notes on the History of Redruth*. J. and M. Roberts, Redruth, 1950.

Nock, O. S. *The Great Western Railway in the Nineteenth Century*. Ian Allan, 1962.

Nock, O. S. *History of the Great Western Railway*, Vols I to III. Ian Allan, 1967.

Oates, A. S. *Around Helston in the Old Days*. Worden & Son, Helston, 1950.

Pearse, Richard. *The Ports and Harbours of Cornwall*. H. E. Warne, 1964.

Roche, T. W. E. *The Withered Arm*. West Country Handbooks, 1967.

Sekon, G. A. *History of the Great Western Railway*. Digby Long & Co, 1895.

Slade, W. J. *Out of Appledore*. Percival Marshall & Co, 1959.

Thomas, David St John. *Double Headed*. David & Charles. 1963.

Thomas, David St John. *A Regional History of the Railways of Great Britain*, Vol I *The West Country*. David & Charles, 1967.

Treanor, Rev T. S. *Heroes of the Goodwin Sands*. Religious Tract Society, 1892.
Underhill, H. A. *Deepwater Sail*. Brown, Son & Ferguson, 1955.
Walling, R. A. J. *The Story of Plymouth*. Westaway Books, 1950.
Whetmath, C. F. D. *The Bodmin and Wadebridge Railway*. West Country Handbooks, 1967.
Woodfin, R. J. *The Centenary of the Cornwall Railway*. W. Jefferson & Son, 1960.
Worth, R. Hansford. *Worth's Dartmoor*. New Edition ed. G. M. Spooner, David & Charles, 1967.

NEWSPAPERS, JOURNALS ETC.

Annual Register, London, 1891.
Belfast Telegraph, 1891.
Coastguard Magazine, various.
Cornishman, 1891.
Cornish Telegraph, 1891.
Dover Express, 1891.
Falmouth Packet, 1891.
GWR *Magazine*, various.
Illustrated London News, 1891.
Lifeboat, Journal of RNLI, various.
Liverpool Daily Post and Echo, 1891.
Lloyd's Universal Register of Shipping, various.
Official Guide to the GWR, 1897.
Old Cornwall, Journal of the Old Cornwall Society, various.
Royal Cornwall Gazette, 1891.
Sea Breezes, various.
The Times, 1891.
West Briton, 1891
Western Morning News, 1891.

ACKNOWLEDGEMENTS

I am indebted to the following people and institutions for their invaluable assistance:

Mr F. Singleton (Meteorological Office, Central Forecasting Office) for his help with the definition of a blizzard, and for his reconstruction of the weather maps for 6–11 March 1891, in terms of the modern concept of frontal analysis. Thanks are also due to the Meteorological Office for making available data contained in the Daily Weather Report at the Meteorological Office Library at Bracknell.

The weather maps for 6–11 March 1891 are based on Crown copyright material by kind permission of the Controller of Her Majesty's Stationery Office.

Miss F. Weekes (Yelverton) for permission to quote from the unpublished account of the blizzard by Mr Frederick Weekes, ARAM.

Mrs J. P. Chadwick (St Kew) for permission to quote from the unpublished account of the blizzard by Miss Rose H. Arundell.

Mr A. C. Crispin (Ogwell), Mrs C. W. Nutt (Fowey) and Mrs I. T. Dixon (Paignton) for loan of contemporary illustrated booklets.

For providing various information:
Capt A. G. Course; Mr J. Salmon (Belfast); Mr J. Behenna (Brixham); Mr J. Horsley (Brixham); Mr F. S. Dunn (Lizard); Mr and Mrs P. F. Mason (Trusham); Dr Whetter (Trispen); Mr R. J. Larn (St Austell).

Acknowledgements

H. L. Douch (curator) and R. Penhallurick (Royal Institution of Cornwall); the staff of Camborne Public Library; the staff of Penzance Public Library; the staff of Plymouth Central Reference Library, Local History Section; the staff of Falmouth Reference Library; the staff of Morrab Library, Penzance.

J. H. Bottrell (*The Cornishman*, Penzance); the staff of *The West Briton*, Truro; I. Hosie (Editor) *The Liverpool Daily Post and Echo;* the staff of *The Dover Express.*

E. H. Fowkes (Archivist, British Transport Historical Records, British Railways Board); C. R. Elliott (Editorial Asistant, Royal National Lifeboat Institution); B. Gallagher (Public Relations Dept, British Railways Western Region); M. K. Stammers (Assistant Keeper of Shipping, City of Liverpool Museums); Miss S. G. Skipper (Assistant Librarian, Board of Trade Marine Library); N. H. Coulter (Drawing Office Manager, Harland & Wolff Ltd, Belfast).

For providing photographs:
R. Barlow (Editor, *The Coastguard*); P. M. Herbert (Bude;); J. Trounson (Redruth); A. Flynn (Truro); F. E. Gibson (Scilly); Helston Borough Museum.

To all those from whose letters and reminiscences I have quoted, I tender my most sincere thanks; regretfully, space does not allow of my naming them individually.

Sancreed,   CLIVE CARTER

Penzance, Cornwall